TOUCHSTONES

For someone like myself who is always looking for words of inspiration, *Touchstones* is a goldmine. Laced with stories from the author's own life experience, the challenges extended to all educators are like an ongoing pebble in the shoe.

Fr Christopher Gleeson SJ
Provincial Delegate for Education and Mission Formation
JCAP Secretary for Secondary Education

The Edmund Rice Charter that Dr Wayne Tinsey speaks about arose out of an experience of the Mystery we call God. Our experience of God is as liberator, all-inclusive, just and with a special preference for people made poor – we have the touchstones of the Charter. Wayne Tinsey has elaborated on this so well and so simply.

Br Philip Pinto CFC
Past Congregation Leader of the Christian Brothers

Wayne is a man of passion with strongly held beliefs from which he would never vary. Two are his commitment to inclusion and social justice. The speeches and the stories woven through this book very much reflect his educational and moral leadership. The book will be of great value to all educators.

Ray Collins
Director of Schools, Diocese of Maitland-Newcastle

Wayne Tinsey's anecdotes, memories and reflections gathered over the years invite his readers to reflect on their own journeys and to see them in a larger horizon of meaningful living and loving.

Professor Maryanne Confoy RSC
Jesuit Theological College, Melbourne

With acuity and humanity Wayne Tinsey reflects on what Catholic schools are today and what they should become in the future. This book poses serious challenges to all who are connected to Catholic schools but it also gives reasons for its author's profound hope for the future.

James B. Nickoloff PhD
Associate Professor Emeritus, Department of Religious Studies, College of the Holy Cross, Worcester, MA
Adjunct Professor of Theology, Barry University, Miami Shores, FL

TOUCH STONES

Stories, Thoughts and Reflections on Catholic Education and the Christian Vision

WAYNE TINSEY

David Lovell Publishing
Melbourne Australia

First published in 2014 by

David Lovell Publishing
PO Box 44, Kew East
Victoria 3102 Australia
tel +61 3 9859 0000
publisher@davidlovellpublishing.com

© Copyright 2014 Wayne Tinsey

This work is copyright. Apart from any fair dealing for the purposes of private study, research, criticism or review, as permitted under the Copyright Act, no part may be reproduced by any process without written permission. Inquiries should be addressed to the publisher.

Front cover photo: binabina/iStock.
Typeset in 12.5/18 Perpetua
This edition printed through Ingram Spark

National Library of Australia Cataloguing-in-Publication data

Touchstones : stories, thoughts and reflections on Catholic education and the Christian vision / Wayne Tinsey.

  ISBN 9781863551755 (paperback)

  Catholic Church – Education – Australia.
  Catholic teachers – Australia – Attitudes.
  Clergy – Australia – Attitudes.

  Tinsey, Wayne, author.

371.071294

touchstone *n.* **1.** a black siliceous stone used to test the purity of gold and silver by the colour of the streak produced on it by rubbing it with either metal. **2.** a test or criterion for the qualities of a thing.

Macquarie Dictionary

**For Danny Hasler
my great mate and inspiration**

*You lived in deeds, not years; thoughts, not breaths;
and made your limited time here an extraordinary
increase in the stock of the world's good.*

*You taught us that excellence is not an act but a habit,
that a meaningful life is mostly lived on the small stage
and is made up of repeated acts of decency and kindness
that add up to something truly magnificant
over the course of a lifetime.*

Contents

Preface   1

Touchstone 1
Education for liberation and the fullness of life   5

Touchstone 2
Education inspired by the Gospel and its priorities   21

Touchstone 3
Education in communities of inclusion   45

Touchstone 4
Education promoting justice and solidarity   63

Leadership and witness: Thoughts for educators   87

Some messages for the young   105

Extract from the
Charter for Catholic Schools
in the Edmund Rice Tradition

All schools and educational entities in the Edmund Rice tradition across Australia are bound by a Charter which identifies four touchstones authentically linked with the charism of Blessed Edmund Rice and which underpin the ministry in our schools and educational endeavours.

A touchstone is a fundamental or quintessential feature of something. As Catholic schools in the Edmund Rice tradition, we aspire to be faithful to the following four touchstones.

Liberating Education

We open hearts and minds, through quality teaching and learning experiences, so that through critical reflection and engagement each person is hope-filled and free to build a better world for all.

Gospel Spirituality

We invite all people into the story of Jesus and strive to make his message of compassion, justice and peace a living reality within our community.

Inclusive Community

Our community is accepting and welcoming, fostering right relationships and committed to the common good.

Justice and Solidarity

We are committed to justice and peace for all, grounded in a spirituality of action and reflection that calls us to stand in solidarity with those who are marginalized and the Earth itself.

(Charter document proclaimed on 22 August 2011)

Preface

The reflections in this collection have their roots in my experience in Catholic education. For most of these 35 years, I have been trying to make deeper sense of what is core to my chosen vocation in a changing context. In many ways the thoughts and musings in this book map my attempts to do this.

The title of the collection and the first four chapters used to group these thoughts relate to the 'Touchstones' that are measures of authenticity in Catholic education in the Edmund Rice tradition. They make great sense to me and I hope they do for you.

Even though these reflections have been arranged under the Touchstones for Edmund Rice Education, they transcend this grouping and can be applied to Catholic education in any context. This has been my experience.

The collection contains two further groupings of thoughts related to the craft of teaching, and some reflections that may speak directly to the young. The grouping is clearly imperfect as many of the pieces could easily fit under several categories.

I have been surprised over the years by the number of people who have expressed interest in these ideas, mainly through my letters and talks, and it is at the request of others that I put them together in this form. My hope is that they might provide a springboard for other people's reflections and search.

Many of these reflections have been with me for so long that I struggle to remember whether they are mine or inspired by something I've read or heard along the way. If I have accidentally taken from other people's work without acknowledging it, I apologize in advance. This is not an academic work and so some of the technicalities of references are not included.

In a real sense I am a 'journeyman' Catholic educator! The old adage that a career path is something better had in hindsight certainly rings true for me. I thank my wife Lita and sons Danny and Carlos for all the traipsing around Australia and the world we have done in the course of this thing that in hindsight I call a career. Had I not had your love, support and trust, my journey would have ended a lot sooner and taken a very different route.

I also take the opportunity to thank the many people who have inspired me in my privileged journey in Catholic education. Many of these I speak about in this book: my heroes from India, Peru and the developing world, and my heroes in life and education. This latter group includes Gustavo Gutierrez, Paolo Freire, Jack Kornfield, Leo Buscaglia, Joan Chittister, Philip Pinto, Barry Dwyer and many others. In a particular way I would like to acknowledge my friend

Michael Elphick. Mick inspired and collaborated with me on several of these reflections. He is a wonderful thinker and a great teacher.

In a special way I offer my deep gratitude to my friends and colleagues in Edmund Rice Education Australia (EREA) and the Christian Brothers. Your support, trust and confidence never cease to inspire and sustain me.

There is an old adage that we are no one until someone believes in us. The Christian Brothers' belief in me allowed me to become a teacher and this belief has never waivered.

Much of the material in this book has been inspired by the Charter for Catholic schools in the Edmund Rice tradition. An extract from this charter is presented in the previous pages. However, these priorities equally apply to all who are involved in the education of our young people. I hope that this Charter will be seen as a source of inspiration for all of us.

TOUCHSTONE 1

Education for liberation and the fullness of life

The capacity to co-create their own versions of the world is a hallmark of the freedom we dream of for the young. To promote and support this journey to liberation, education must often adopt a counter-cultural stance to our society and its priorities. Questions of ultimate importance are asked and there is necessary suspicion of the easy answers on offer. The Christian promise of deep meaning and fullness of life awaits.

A fire for life

Jesus says of his mission: 'I have come that they may have life, and have it to the full.' This theme is surely central to our tradition. Christian faith is much more than affirmation of a particular creed or set of truths. It is a commitment to, a stance or posture towards life.

A turning point in my career as a teacher came several years ago when I learned that a former student of mine committed suicide. This girl had been in my religion and homeroom classes for two years. I remember her as a pretty and intelligent girl but a loner who had a somewhat troubled home life. At the age of 21, having just graduated from university, she drove herself to a quiet park in Sydney, locked the doors of her car and ended her life.

When I heard of this girl's death I was reminded of a question once posed by American educator Leo Buscaglia — a question that I'm sure all educators ask at some time in their careers: 'What does it matter that we teach young people to read, write and do arithmetic, when we can't teach them vital lessons on life's sacredness, meaning and purpose?' To what avail were my religion lessons when this girl didn't pick up a sense of the beauty of her own personhood? As Yeats once said, 'Education is not filling a bucket but lighting a fire.' Surely this fire should translate into a passion for life, meaning and purpose!

Buscaglia suggests that we run the risk of teaching everything in the world to our young except the most essential thing: the essence of full, creative and lived humanity. We assume that young people learn this by osmosis. But when we look around at our fragmented world, it doesn't appear to be working that well by osmosis alone.

Education for full humanity

Psychologist Haim Ginott, citing a letter written by a Holocaust survivor to educators, wrote:

> I am a survivor of a concentration camp. My eyes have seen what no person should witness. Gas chambers built by learned engineers and children poisoned by educated physicians. Infants killed by trained nurses. Women and babies shot and killed by high school and college graduates. Oh I am suspicious of education. My only request is, help your students to be human. Our efforts should never produce learned monsters, skilled psychopaths, educated Eichmanns. Reading, writing and spelling and arithmetic are only important when they serve to make our students human.

The guiding intent for all education should be 'humanization', in the fullest sense of the word. Should we assume that the education we prescribe for our young people prepares them not only for a complex and changing world but also how to relate to other human beings? What about happiness and enjoyment of living? What about courage and the conquest of fear? What about peace of mind, the ability to give and receive love? What of confidence, self-respect and self-discipline? What about hope for the future and contentment in later years?

As Leo Buscaglia proposes, our kids will be only half educated unless they have acquired a sense of human dignity and worth, an appreciation of life, the knowledge of how to use their limited time wisely, and the determination to leave the world a better place for their having been in it.

Salvation

Christian mission implies participating in God's offer of life and salvation for the whole world, a world which craves this life and salvation. 'Saved from what?' one of my students once asked during a religion class. The Gospel teaches that we can be saved from meaninglessness and purposelessness. This is Good News in an age of pessimism and anxiety. It's particularly Good News for our young, many of whom are perishing through lack of meaning and purpose in their lives.

Freedom must be claimed

At the end of apartheid, Nelson Mandela warned his people that they were not yet free; that they had merely achieved the possibility for freedom. I think he was implying that true freedom is something that must be actively claimed by each person.

The Brazilian educator Paolo Freire argued that education must help every individual to win back the right to say his or her own word and name the world they live in. One of the central concerns of Christian education should be to equip young people to critique their reality, to awaken in them a sense that they need not be passive and to claim what is surely a basic human right: the capacity to make meaning for themselves. In a world where values of justice and equity have been abandoned in favour of the values of markets, education then becomes the practice of liberation.

The critique of culture

For many young people in our culture, meaning in key areas of their lives is imposed on them in such a way that they cannot and do not question it. They are not free. Meaning is packaged for many people in our society. As Michael Warren once wrote: 'It is not the culture of the people but the culture concocted for the people's consumption!'

Barry Dwyer wrote of the role of Catholic schooling in responding to our dominant culture. In his words, we must 'identify and celebrate the humanizing and ennobling elements within it, and offer the Gospel's alternatives to those definitions of reality that oppress and enslave the human spirit.'

As parents and Christian educators, we aim to form young people who can undertake the production of meaning themselves, first by becoming questioners of the products handed to them for consumption and then by becoming co-creators of their own versions of the world. A possible mission statement for schools and families alike.

The hero

The Greek roots of the word suggest that the hero is *one who can choose*. The heroic journey is often counter-cultural as the hero interprets life through her or his own experience. The journey leads to questioning and interrogation of the culture in which one lives. Who am I? What is valuable? How do I find peace and happiness? What does it mean to live justly? These questions disturb the hero, who is suspicious of the easy answers that are readily on offer in the dominant culture. Our Catholic schools are in the business of creating heroes! An exciting thought!

Love people – use things

As educators we are consistently made aware that the young people we care for live in a culture where things can be valued over people, where having can be valued above giving and success can sometimes be limited to how much we accumulate. In a talk some years ago, Jesuit Fr Jim Di Giacomo proposed that consumerism is different from Christianity in one very important way. 'Christianity teaches us to love people and use things. Consumerism teaches us to love things and to use people!'

Clearly, most facets of the culture described above are not intrinsically bad or destructive to the human spirit. It is when all other values are subordinate to those aspired to by the consumer society and when people uncritically assimilate this view of what the good and responsible life is, that consumerism is most destructive. The vehicle of consumerism is advertising, and advertising tells us that our highest calling is to be consumers, that happiness can be bought, that products can fulfil us and satisfy our deepest human needs.

To be more, not have more

I was teaching in the inner city of Sydney in the late 1980s. A Year 9 physical education student of mine attended one class out of ten in the school term, always having some excuse for not participating. When his mother approached me at parent-teacher night to discuss her son's fail grade in the subject, a sad and disturbing truth emerged. In that boy's peer group, your whole sense of self-worth and identity was dictated by the brand of running shoes you had. To be anyone of worth you needed to wear certain designer brands. This boy's family could only afford cheaper shoes, so, rather than be seen wearing them by his peers, he sacrificed a whole term's education. When I relate this story to fellow educators, they often speak of similar incidents from their experience.

Pope John Paul II urged that 'we must help our young people to *be* more, not have more.' As educators or parents, we have a very significant role in guiding young people towards seeking what is of lasting significance in life. This can often call us towards a counter-cultural stance when it comes to our dominant culture's vision of what is important and what is meaningful.

Equanimity and freedom of heart

Roberto de Vincenzo was an Argentine golfer who became quite famous in the 1960s. He was the first golfer from South America to make it on the big stage.

There is a famous story told of the time Roberto won a golf tournament and received his large prize cheque. In those days, professional golfers drove themselves from tournament to tournament, and he was in the car park about to put his golf clubs in the boot of his car when he was approached by a woman who had a baby in her arms. She said, 'Mr de Vincenzo, my baby is very sick and will die if he does not receive the right medicine. Can you please help me?'

Without hesitation, Roberto de Vincenzo signed his winning cheque over to the woman, saying to her, 'There you go, lady. I hope your child enjoys many happy days.'

A week later, as he arrived at another PGA tournament, an official came up to him and said, 'Roberto, I hear that you handed over your winner's cheque last week to a lady who had a sick baby.' 'Yes', he said, 'that's right'. The official said, 'I'm sorry, my friend, but she fleeced you. The lady was a fraud and the baby was not sick.' Roberto responded, 'You mean there was no sick baby who was going to die?' 'Yes', said the official. Roberto responded, 'Well that's the best news I've heard all year!'

Through his response, Roberto de Vincenzo demonstrated wonderful equanimity and freedom of heart. His reaction was that of a truly free person.

Free for the good

A truly liberating education will lead our young people to a deep freedom of heart: to the realisation that liberty is not a licence to do whatever you want but the freedom to do what you ought to. Pope Francis recently put it this way:

> Liberty means to be able to reflect on what we do, to know how to appreciate what is good and what is bad, to choose always the good. We are free for the good.

The sooner our young people can come to understand that happiness, in reality, is always closer to acceptance and contentment than it is to pleasure, the happier they will be – and also the more liberated they will be in the way they see the world and their place in it. Happiness abides in a compassionate heart. If our hearts are focused on the deepest values of the Kingdom of God, rules and regulations almost become redundant. A compassionate, warm and generous heart will always strive to do what is right.

Responsibility for 'the other'

I sometimes listen to the work of motivational gurus on tapes and CDs. In the main I find their work very helpful. However, they often make the claim that we all have the capacity to change our life by changing how we feel about a particular scenario we find ourselves in. This promise will come as cold comfort to the people in Bangladesh or Africa who are struggling to find enough food for their families. It will also be cold comfort for the people in India who because of caste have been born with no rights and their family will suffer a similar fate.

We need to teach our young that their search for meaning and full humanity should not come at the expense of other people. Our capacity to achieve fullness of life is linked to our combined responsibility to bring about the fullness of possibility for the whole of humankind.

And yet not everyone is born with the same possibility to achieve their full potential and so there is a need for responsibility for the 'other'. We need to teach them that, whether we like it or not, whether we even know it or not, the destinies of all people on this earth are intricately entwined. In this sense, we are all brothers and sisters.

Two 'gospels' – true freedom

All individuals and institutions that take their mission from Christ are being asked to balance two conflicting gospels: Jesus' essential message of Good News and liberation for the world on one hand, and the gospel of the dominant, pluralist society on the other. Individuals and institutions that take their basic orientation from Christianity are being challenged to reassess how they balance the conflicting messages of these two revelation systems.

The conflict of these gospels brings a distorted view of what it means to be truly free in contemporary society. Young people stress their need for individualism and freedom but are often unconsciously slaves to fashion, advertising and the mandates of consumerism.

I witnessed an interview with a young Muslim woman who chose to wear a veil and moderate form of Islamic dress to her classes at Sydney University. When the interviewer implied that somehow the wearing of the dress was restricting her freedom, she replied that she felt truly free since she chose to dress according to her beliefs. She added that she pitied the lack of freedom she witnessed in her fellow students who appeared to be slaves to fashion and peer group pressure.

Shining light on the darkness of mere being

(Reflections shortly after the tragic death of young Elliot Fletcher at the hands of another student at St Patrick's College, Shorncliffe, in 2010.)

The circumstances surrounding Elliot's death constitute a deep human tragedy beyond comprehension. On the surface, we could justifiably say that there can be nothing positive in this tragedy; everyone loses. How is meaning made in the context of such a tragedy? Is it possible to reflect on what happened that week and rescue anything that can give us hope in the future?

Carl Jung once said that 'the point of human life is to shine light on the darkness of mere being.' How has this extraordinary human spirit shone through in the response to Elliot's death? In this tragedy, how has the glory of God shone through in the deeply human responses of this community?

Our thoughts and prayers were immediately with Elliot's mum and dad. We realise that there is no inherent gene or resource that prepares one to outlive one's child. It is a pain beyond our imagining, and survival means drawing on resources that few would see themselves as having. Yet, in the midst of their pain and grief,

Elliot's parents' prime concern was for the wellbeing of the other boys at St Pat's. How were they coping with this? Such wonderful compassion in the face of crippling grief is surely a triumph of the human spirit.

As staff and leaders in schools, we can probably anticipate that at certain times we will face tragedy. We will have to cope with road accident fatalities; deaths of students resulting from accident or illness; and, given the way our society is moving, we might even have to cope with the suicide of a student. But there is absolutely nothing that can prepare a leader or a staff for what happened at St Pat's that week. The extraordinary way in which Michael Carroll, his staff and his board responded, their care for their community, their concern for the boys and for the families involved — all have been a great triumph for the human spirit in the worst of circumstances.

There were other 'triumphs' that perhaps weren't as noticed. I witnessed a car pull up at the front gate of St Pat's after school on the day after Elliot's death. Out of the car stepped a mum and her two sons about the same age as Elliot. It wasn't a flash car and the family was of humble means. One of the boys had a bunch of flowers in his hand. As they approached the gate of the school, they were welcomed and asked if they were friends of Elliot's. The mum answered that they didn't know Elliot, but in their discussions over breakfast they were so overcome with compassion that they felt they had to do something.

This family had driven over an hour and a half through the

traffic and rain of that Brisbane afternoon to deliver some flowers at the gate of the school, because of the compassion they felt and the human need to express it. The compassion of this family and thousands of others like them is testimony to the triumph of the human spirit!

Throughout the week, there was enormous support, prayers and concern for both families directly involved. The community did not forget the other family involved in this tragedy. One of the most disturbing images to come out of that week was the thought of a young boy who is in prison at the moment. How terrified must he be? What must be going on in his mind and what must the pain of his mum be like as they try to come to terms with what is happening in their lives? The recognition that this is a deep tragedy for *all* involved is a triumph for human compassion in a world that is quick to blame and eager to find scapegoats.

This community is doing everything possible to learn from what happened that tragic week and is using these lessons to increase in the boys and the whole community a deeper sense of what it means to 'shine light on the darkness of mere being'. They do this in the light of our Christian faith and prove that the human spirit does have the potential to make meaning and sense of the world, even in the most senseless of times. The light will prevail and the human spirit will surely triumph.

Freedom for the Gospel

Edmund Rice Education Australia (EREA) is blessed to be able to forge its identity within the context of a broad vision serving the Reign of God. This gives us a broad canvas and much freedom to claim its identity within the church. Yes, we work with and for our local church; however, we claim the freedom of the congregation that has a broad, international focus and clear priority in ministry for those at the margins of society.

This freedom we enjoy can only be legitimately claimed in service of the Gospel. As we resist ideological positions that threaten to constrain us, we must be careful not to create our own ideologies. As inspiring and powerful as the story of Edmund might be, we must always remind one another that it is, in essence, only a lens into the bigger story of the one who both inspired and sustained Edmund Rice. The Gospel, with its challenges and its promises, must remain the core focus of our mission and our identity.

TOUCHSTONE 2

Education inspired by the Gospel and its priorities

Catholic schools must be places where who we are and what we try to do is permeable to and inspired by the priorities of the Christian Gospel. Our policies, our relationships, our inclusivity, what we see as being important, what we celebrate, who we serve, what we challenge, all need to be guided by the priorities of the Gospel.

Our fruits and our roots

It is a reality that many of our schools have become comfortable and attractive to those who, in the words of Dominican researcher Carmel Leavey, may primarily seek our 'fruits but not our roots'.

In some cases we have become schools of choice for people who aspire to a version of exclusive, private education. In a society that increasingly sees education as a commodity that can be bought, we must resist the temptation to have our schools used principally as vehicles for socio-differentiation and creeping elitism. Where does this leave us when the Gospel tells us that our mission should focus on serving the materially poor?

Defining success

At times, the parents of our students need to be reminded that we are on about more than strong academic results, good discipline and providing a caring environment, as important as these qualities are for any school community. To set our priorities and define our success solely by league tables and sporting achievements betrays the foundations upon which we stand.

We must challenge versions of the world that define success solely in terms of money, accumulation of things and over-emphasis on status and security. Our aim is to equip young people to critique our consumer culture and its version of the good, the well-lived, the important and a meaningful life. How well we do this should become our guide to authenticity, our measure of success.

Regrettably, some voices in the church say that Catholic education has passed its 'golden era', and that Catholic schools increasingly lack relevance in the church's mission. There may be some validity in these claims if Catholic schools are being driven by agendas that cannot be linked to the Gospel but rather by economic rationalist thinking and by the 'gods' of the HSC, TEE and VCE. If the thing that we can boast most proudly about to the world is our ability to get good tertiary entrance rankings out of the students, then perhaps our schools should be closed or at least renamed to more honestly reflect these aims and aspirations.

This is not an attack on the pursuit of academic excellence: rather it is a call for honesty and authenticity. Let us be guided by the words of Archbishop Oscar Romero of El Salvador, who, shortly before he was killed, reminded his people: 'Judge not your success by your numbers or the quality of your buildings ... judge your success by the quality of your hearts and your efforts to live the call of the Gospel.'

Let us not measure the excellence of our school only by its buildings or by its academic results. What really matters is you, this community and your hearts: God's grace giving you truth and life, and you offering this as gift to the world!

Heralds of the Kingdom

We in schools are ministers of the Christian Gospel; heralds of the Reign of God. We work within a church that, sadly, has lost much of its moral authority in our culture. With the proliferation of sexual abuse scandals and the general decline of formal religion in the West, the church's capacity to speak truth with authority has been seriously compromised. It is from this position of humility and brokenness that we offer our vision for what constitutes the life well lived. When people are losing faith in an institutional church, who will speak for the Reign of God if it isn't the people who've been given the privilege of education?

A movement not an institution

Although they may be disengaged from the institutional church, most young people do want to be part of a movement that will inspire them and engage their imagination. Like you, I have taught so many young people who have rejected a church they judge to be out of touch, but I have taught very few whose imagination and passion haven't been captured by a prophet who spoke to his reality, who championed the excluded and who offers meaning to a life of possibility.

The 'little man'

Some years ago, while travelling in India, I stopped at a roadside bazaar that sold souvenirs. The seller, presumably a Hindu, had various religious pieces for sale, including a beautifully carved wooden cross. I expressed some interest, but, as I was about to move on and not buy, the man said: 'Perhaps, sir, you would be interested in a similar one I have in my other store. Just as beautiful but it costs a little more because it has a little man on it!' This was an amusing scene and what the seller didn't understand is that it is the 'little man', the human person of Jesus on the cross, that makes all the difference to Christians.

In our quest to educate for full humanity and liberation, we introduce the young to Jesus, who showed that it was possible to be fully human through passionate engagement in this world. Jesus' acceptance of the human condition gives enormous dignity to our humanity and affirms the sacredness of the ordinary person.

The clarity of mystery

As educators, we deal with information, knowledge and wisdom. In Catholic education, we also deal with mystery. In considering the relationship between them, T. S. Eliot once asked, 'Where is the knowledge that is lost in information, where is the wisdom that is lost in knowledge?'

Our modern world is desperately seeking leadership in identifying what is of lasting importance. Our culture values the acquisition, organization, and dissemination of facts, more than it does the getting of wisdom, which Ram Dass suggests 'requires the emptying and quiet opening of the mind, the application of the heart, and the alchemy of reason and feeling.' This surely is the stuff of Catholic education!

Joan Chittister put it this way:

> We know far too much and, in the knowing, find ourselves perceiving far too little. We have developed one-dimensional souls, awash with facts, bereft of the clarity of mystery.

Let us reflect a while on what she means by the 'clarity of mystery'. In a society where our sense of reality can be limited by what we perceive through our senses, this is a very strange concept indeed.

Affirming personhood

My family and I once had the privilege of spending Christmas with a leper community in a city south of Kolkata. For my family it was the first engagement with sufferers of leprosy. Prior to taking my wife and two sons into the leper colony, I prepared them as best I could for some of the confronting and difficult sights they might encounter. At one point I said to them that in my opinion you've never shaken anyone's hand until you've shaken the hand of someone with leprosy.

Upon arrival at the colony, I took the family into the dispensary where some of the worst cases are initially treated before they find their way in the community. In the course of being introduced to these patients, most of whom had stark wounds and amputations, my wife and sons not only reached out to shake hands, but they embraced many of the patients and engaged with them in a very natural way. Of course, I was enormously proud of them!

Later on we discussed the full significance of what had happened in that encounter. When we shake hands in our culture it's most often a gesture between equals. However, as I explained to my sons, the moment we reach out and touch someone who has leprosy, it may be the first time in that person's life that they've been afforded the dignity of being considered a human being worthy of touch. In their world they are considered outcasts and unable to take any place in society. They would not normally encounter human touch on a regular basis outside their family. To have someone reach out and embrace them can be a profound acknowledgement of their humanity.

Even though we may never encounter a person with leprosy or any other such extreme marginalization, as Christians we are all called to affirm and champion human dignity and potential and include the excluded.

Light on life

As human institutions, we can only struggle to live up to our own vision, to reform our life continually, so as to be consistent with our vision. Our efforts to address these questions in the light of the Gospel contribute to our authenticity and capacity to claim the title of Christian education. Faithfulness to the Gospel demands that we do so.

Our claims of authenticity will always be flawed unless they are based on the Gospel's capacity to add meaning and purpose to human life. Let us take our opportunity to prove that religious inspiration has the capacity to add value to the human search for meaning and purpose and to motivate service and inclusion.

Let us recover our voice and, taking inspiration from John Kennedy's famous words, find the contribution that this particular generation of Catholic education leaders can make to the future by educating for the Reign of God with passion and urgency. Jon Sobrino warns of the consequences of not doing so when he states, 'A church shrivels up and dies if it fails to shed light on people's lives!' Let us hope that this will not happen on our watch!

Gratitude and blessings

Last week I learned a valuable lesson about valuing and appreciating the small things in life. This experience brought home to me the meaning of the ancient Persian saying: 'I wept because I had no shoes, until I saw a person with no feet!'

I was in India with a group of 16 people from our schools and we were about to visit a community of people who suffer from leprosy. At the entrance to the colony, we encountered a woman who had a very badly advanced case of leprosy and found it very difficult to walk. She greeted us with a smile and was very excited.

We found out that this woman had travelled for four hours to reach the colony so that she could receive a pair of sandals fashioned especially for people with leprosy, made from discarded truck and car tyres. Since people with leprosy lose the feeling in their limbs, stronger protection is necessary, particularly on the feet, so that they don't suffer from infection caused by cuts to the feet and other abrasions.

I visited the small workshop in the colony where these rough sandals were made and I found the same woman in an overwhelmingly happy and excited state of mind. I spoke with the cobbler and he showed me the sandals the lady was about to receive. I have to admit that I was taken aback when I first saw them, as the left foot seemed to be normal size whereas the right was only big enough to cover the stump this lady had where her foot used to be. But I was privileged to see the delight and thankfulness she expressed when she was presented with this basic footwear. It was like she had won the lottery!

Not far from my house in Melbourne there is a very expensive shoe shop where people can pay $1000 and upwards for a pair of imported shoes. I wonder how long I would have to observe the happenings in that shop to encounter anyone expressing anything near the delight this woman showed at the receipt of her simple sandals. In fact, I've seen some fairly angry and disappointed looks on the faces of people simply because the half size is not available or the shoe doesn't quite fit or they have to wait for service.

Perhaps we can all learn a lesson from this simple woman about being thankful and rejoicing in the simple blessings we receive. As Eric Hoffer once said, 'The hardest arithmetic to master is that which enables us to count our blessings.'

New wineskins

In the Gospel of St Mark, Jesus speaks of the need for new, flexible wineskins to store the new wine of the Kingdom of God. There was tension between the new wine of the Kingdom of God that Jesus preached and some of the existing rigid religious structures. This new vision of Jesus cracked the brittle skins of some of the Sadducees, Pharisees and scribes. When considering this story, it is important to remember that the wine is the essential substance; the skins are secondary. We can't drink the skins, they are only important because they store the wine.

Philosopher Jaroslav Pelikan proposed that 'Tradition is the living faith of the dead; traditionalism is the dead faith of the living. It is traditionalism that gets tradition a bad name!' As another thinker puts it: 'The Christian position is never one of static conformance to dead rules, but of dynamic obedience to a living God!' As great as the past may have been, we have an obligation to forge an even better future. Over-reliance on 'tradition' can see the perpetuation of old patterns of the past without questioning their relevance. This is 'traditionalism' and it stifles the prophetic.

Christian tradition is the timeless collective community experience of God. It is the faith that has been lived out in the church since the time of the apostles. Our tradition grounds our faith in human experience. It speaks to the challenges of our times and is essential to evangelization and dialogue. However, tradition should not be confused with traditionalism, which is uncritical of past practice and suggests that almost all past practices are necessary for fidelity, even though they may not speak to the present-day reality.

Faith, beliefs and tradition

The tradition of faith is always tolerant of and enhanced by change and difference and is characterized by fluidity and dialogue. New Zealand theologian Lloyd Geering proposed that

> Jeremiah and Augustine and Martin Luther didn't have the same beliefs at all, but they're all people of faith, great faith,

and they belong to a tradition of faith. That is why the Judeo-Christian tradition which is now some 4000 years old, has a continuity in it, running through it, and yet it is changing to meet the needs of the cultural environment through which it is passing.

Referring further to the tradition of faith in varying contexts of time and culture, Geering uses the analogy of a river running through the fields of time 'gathering things from the banks as it's going along and also dropping things and so on. What is permanent is simply the continuity of the river rather than what is in it. With the flow of the river, the water even changes.' Contact with new and diverse cultures and contexts enriches the tradition of faith, which, by definition, is never static and unchanging.

Educators and parents know that many young and not so young people appear to be rejecting 'the Faith'. I'm sure that this is not a rejection of the power the Christian vision has to make a difference in their lives, or even of Christ, but a rejection of the forms in which the package of faith is presented to them. The principal purpose of the church is to transmit Christian meanings and the eternal message of God's love, not the preservation of traditional cultural forms. Specific beliefs and practices are vehicles that should be assessed, altered and, if necessary, updated, to ensure the preservation of this transmission. It is the content of Christian faith, not the form in which it was originally or has been traditionally expressed, that is sacred.

The new wine of the Kingdom challenges us all to move beyond our rigid positions and become more open to the possibilities brought by an *ongoing incarnation*. Let us pray that we will not become brittle like the old skins and lose the precious essence of our living tradition. Those of us who work with youth are constantly challenged to become more open in our dialogue on church, mission and what is truly important and essential for happiness, and to become more faithful to the Christian vision that is both ancient and ever new.

A church 'enfleshed' in culture

In the post-Vatican II church, evangelization needs to be understood as dialogue with culture. The Gospel is always 'enfleshed' or 'embodied' in a people. In this paradigm, it is not so much a case of the church being expanded through evangelization, but of the church being born anew in each new context and culture.

Some 20 years ago, I attended a lecture in Sydney that had a profound influence on my own vision for church and mission. The speaker, whose name now escapes me, was a Canadian White Father (Missionary of Africa) who had worked in Africa for 30 years.

He began by saying that, after being ordained a priest in Canada, he immediately boarded a ship bound for Africa. There he was met at the dock, given a short period of time to get his bearings, and sent to a village to begin work. As the dominant model of mission in those days dictated, the entire measure of the success or failure of his work was how many conversions or baptisms he made.

He lived with the people of that village for a period of years. They loved him and he loved them. They cared for him when he was sick and struggling to come to terms with life in his new home. He told them his stories of Jesus. But, at the end of five years, when he and his bishop were assessing the success of his ministry, he realized that he had had very few conversions to Christianity. He decided that he was perhaps in need of a move if he was going to be successful in ministry. The bishop agreed and organized a move for him. When he told the people, they were very sad that he was leaving. What they said changed his whole concept of church and ministry.

They said words to the effect of, 'Father, you should know our culture pretty well by now. You should know that for thousands of years the teaching authority and wisdom in things related to religion and spirituality come down through the elders. Father, you are a very young man!'

And they also said to him, 'Father, you know that in our culture a man is not considered a man until he has had his first son. Father, you don't even have a wife!' The priest said that hearing these and similar things from these people, whom he loved and respected, marked a real Copernican change in his thinking about his priesthood and ministry in this culture.

He realized that if the message and truth of the Gospel of Jesus Christ was going to take root in this culture, he was going to have to let go of many of the cultural trappings that came with being European or Canadian, Australian or Irish. In Africa, or anywhere, the essential core of the message of Jesus Christ is relevant and has transformative power. However, responses to the Gospel and possible subsequent expressions of church, were necessarily going to look different from the type of church that he had come to Africa hoping to establish. After reassessing the criteria laid down to assess his success or failure, the priest stayed on in that village for several years.

Simplistic measures of success

Sadly, there are those who judge the success or failure of Catholic education by simplistic measures such as Mass attendance or lack of attendance. The decline in practice among young people leads them to question the relevance and future of Catholic education. An example of this simplistic logic is the scathing assessment of the effectiveness of Catholic education in Melbourne in 2001 by a contributor to a Catholic journal who wrote, 'Only 6% of 18-24 year-olds attend Mass on any sort of regular basis. We could say that Catholic schools in Melbourne have a 94% failure rate.'

For advocates of this view, evangelization and ministry can be nervous activities aimed primarily at church expansion and maintenance. There is nothing intrinsically wrong with these aims, but surely the freedom of Vatican II, the complexity of our world and the reality and needs of our kids, call for an expanded vision for church and evangelization that must urgently dialogue with culture and speak to our youth.

I would suggest that people whose vision for evangelization and mission is reflected in the previous paragraphs should be urged to leave or stay out of ministry, particularly with youth. The current context is too complex for simplistic, exclusive and rigid approaches, however well intentioned they may be.

A hope-filled vision

In one of his books, Fr Gerry Arbuckle refers to a statement from the World Council of Churches, and this piece really speaks to me as an educator who believes in the future. It advises:

> Ministry should never become a nervous effort to keep people in or win them for the church. A style of life that is inspired by the Gospel and a genuine care for a new generation is all that is required. The message of the Good News is strong enough to excite, engage and commit those of all ages.

I wonder how many of us really believe this. Viktor Frankl discovered in his internment in the Nazi death camps that the key to survival was not the physical strength of the person but their ability to maintain hope. Are we hopeful about the future of the church?

A Kingdom-centred community needs to be a community of

hope. Negativism and pessimism have no place because they betray a lack of faith. Of course, hope must be proactive. We pray after the Lord's Prayer at Mass that we are spared needless anxiety because we have hope.

Cardinal Suenens described a 'hope-filled' spirituality which fits beautifully with what I have been endeavouring to say:

> I have hope because I believe that God is born anew each morning, because I believe that God is creating the world at this very moment in time. It is happening now. We must be ready to expect the unexpected from God. God is here, near us, unforeseeable and loving. I believe the Holy Spirit is at work in the church and in the world, even where the name of God is unheard. I believe in the surprises of the Holy Spirit. To hope is a duty, not a luxury. To hope is not to dream, but to turn dreams into reality.

What defines us

Many Catholic schools belong to external sporting associations and historically this has been encouraged as a way of promoting healthy competition and moving the school's standing forward. We must always remember, however, that belonging to external associations is what we do, not who we are! Only our core business and deepest sense of mission should define us, nothing else. We are not PSA, GPS or APS schools: we are all Catholic schools with all that that implies!

The core of charism

Many Catholic schools celebrate the charism of the religious congregation they were founded by. Often times we hear this word 'charism', but what does it really mean?

For me:

- A charism is a particular lens into the Gospel story; the vision and experience of one person shedding light on the core priorities of Jesus.
- It is an indicator of 'true north' in our attempts for greater authenticity in mission.
- No individual or group 'owns' a charism. It is a gift to be shared and grown, not nervously guarded.
- A charism should never be a source of comfort, but rather something that always disturbs into new growth and understanding of the Gospel vision.
- A charism brings a sense of unity; it defines our identity, the face we wish to show to the world.
- A charism clearly serves the Gospel; it is never a replacement for the Gospel. It always points towards the Kingdom of God; always striving for the creation of a better world and deeper humanity.
- A charism should never be a tool for triumphalism or complacency; it is constantly in need of revision in the face of the 'signs of the times', the needs of our world; in that sense it is never static or fixed but always evolving.

A charism, in short, defines what our central priorities must always be — our deepest values.

Live fully — love well

We all know that we should not have to wait for a moment when we face our mortality front on, for example, through sickness or loss, to re-evaluate what is truly important in our lives. We get only one chance at life. Nothing is ours but time. We have a responsibility to make the most of the time we have here. While everyone dies, not everyone really lives. Each day, each hour, each minute needs to be a new beginning.

As golf legend Ben Hogan said, 'As you walk down the fairway of life, you must smell the roses, for you only get to play one round.' In the end, when we look at our life, perhaps the questions will be simple:

Did I live fully?

Did I love well?

Ancient Egyptians believed that upon their death they would be asked by the gods two questions and their answers would determine whether they could continue their journey in the afterlife. The first question was, 'Did you bring joy?' The second was, 'Did you find joy?' These goals then become a sacred charge in life and the only way to obtain eternal happiness.

The tough questions

We must not let fear, attachment to the past or seduction by other agendas deter us from being single-minded in our commitment to a vision for Catholic education in which we proclaim education as liberation, as a means of experiencing full humanity and the vehicle of 'good news' to those who are at the margins of our society. Let us continue to challenge one another and have those difficult conversations as we journey into deeper authenticity. To do anything less is to betray the mission we have been given and the foundations upon which we stand.

Let us with renew our commitment to a vision for excellence that is broad and inclusive of those core human elements of education that are not easily measured. A vision for excellence that gives priority to authenticity in mission reflected in our passion for the Gospel and commitment to promoting service and the common good above individual advancement as the highest aspirations for our youth. A vision for excellence that empowers young people to critique and become co-creators of their world.

Philip Pinto, Congregation Leader of the Christian Brothers, once said that we must be prepared to lead our young down new paths, since many of the old have become toxic. Our efforts must prepare our young to speak for the poor and excluded, lest the inhuman cycle continue for another generation. We need to teach them to question and critique our world, not simply inhabit it. As Joan Chittister reminds us, 'It's not the answers we teach them to give, but rather it's the questions we teach them to ask, that are the measure of the spiritual leadership we give to the emerging generation.'

Today we face tough questions around inclusivity based on gender and sexual orientation, as well as our commitment to education for the sustainability of our planet. Some of our responses to date have been and remain inadequate. May these questions continue to challenge and ground us; may we avoid complacency and becoming insulated from issues that demand a Gospel-centred response.

Radical for the Kingdom

Our current plight requires us to be radical — radical in the sense of going back to the roots, the original sense of the term — trying to recapture something of what excited Jesus, something of the preoccupation of the Kingdom.

It is up to us how far we want to go. We can opt for a safe, a moderate expression of the Christian vision, or we can opt for something far more powerful, more explicit and more radical. I hope that the basis of our decision never becomes how much we are about the institution in contrast to how much we are about the Kingdom. This would be a sad betrayal of the very ideals for which many of us embarked on this Christian journey and on this journey in Catholic education.

The counter-cultural message

The Christian Gospel presents an essentially counter-cultural message on many issues in today's world. There should be a certain tension between the Christian's religious beliefs and the wider culture. The former must challenge the latter. The Christian Church is charged with being the leaven in society. The credibility of the church's message is measured by its engagement in the social area.

The Christian Church needs and wants to be relevant and credible. Awareness alone is insufficient. Unless the church becomes a producer of meaning, its discernment will remain passive. As Pope John Paul, in a letter to the Pontifical Council on Culture, said, 'A faith that does not become culture is … not fully lived out. Other voices in society will be only too willing to offer our youth their perspectives on life, success and meaning if the church can't or doesn't.

Gospel-centredness

Essential to the evangelization process are the clear articulation and grounding of the Gospel's potential to shed light on the deep human, existential and spiritual questions faced by all cultures throughout history. Christian insights into the quest for God and full humanity are given priority. The hearer is invited to spiritual growth, conversion to God and the priorities of the Gospel. This is a movement towards 'people of God-ness'. Conversion leads to an ongoing and ever deepening reorientation of both individual and community, to Gospel-centredness.

This conversion is not getting a membership into a club, or changing a religious preference, not even joining a religious organization: it is becoming a disciple of Jesus. Conversion is turning towards Jesus in a radical way, accepting the responsibilities of Christian discipleship and taking over responsibility for the bringing of the Reign of God.

TOUCHSTONE 3

Education in communities of inclusion

Jesus was clearly the 'great includer'! Inclusion was a defining feature of his ministry and ultimately brought him into the conflict that led to his death. Women, children, lepers, those from other communities — all experience an inclusion that led them to new life. As followers of Jesus, our authenticity must surely be defined by those we dare to include.

We teach each other

To the parents, guardians and community elders of the Aboriginal and Torres Strait Islander students of our schools, I thank you for entrusting your children to us. We will do all that we can to care for them and teach them in a way that enables their gifts and talents to emerge and thrive. We will also endeavour to educate them in accord with the values and principles of the Christian Gospel. These values, that include forgiveness, reconciliation and inclusion, both inspire and challenge us. Never has the embracing of these values by all been so vital for our world and its survival.

I also ask that you teach not only your own children but ours as well. Urgently, we ask that you teach us a sense of the sacred. Unfortunately, in Western society, we have been very good at separating what we label as 'sacred' and what we see as 'secular' or ordinary. We have compartmentalized religion and spirituality into a certain section of our lives, both privately and in our broader culture. For many people it is a part of their life that fits into one particular hour on one particular day of the week. We keep religion and spirituality separate from the day-to-day business of our lives.

However, for you, the First Peoples of our nation, the world is sacred. There is no distinction between religion and life. Everything around you speaks of the spirit. I strongly believe that the future of our world depends on emerging generations rediscovering a sense of the sacred in everything and the awe and reverence towards life that this evokes. You have much to teach us in this regard.

The most powerful lessons

I acknowledge my indebtedness to the nameless people of the developing world, in particular India, for the formation I have received which prepares me to speak today. I have learned more about life, the Reign of God and mission from my time with these people than I ever did in formal university studies.

In India I have learned that authenticity in Catholic schooling has little to do with the numbers of Catholics we have enrolled or the standard of our buildings. I have learned that inclusion is at the heart of the Gospel and exclusion is its greatest betrayal. I have learned that a school's capacity to make a difference is not simply dependent on its physical resources but on humble resolve within the community to build the Reign of God and embrace solidarity with the excluded ones.

The lessons from inclusion

Some Catholic schools speak of their mission as one of education of the 'elite', the future lawmakers and leaders in our society, in an environment where Christian values and social justice are emphasized. There is no doubt that this can make a valuable contribution to the future. However, how much more powerful can the formation of these future leaders be if their education takes place in a context of social inclusion and equity, in a school community representative of broader society, where the values we hope they will embrace in future leadership for a better world are present in the daily reality of their school days. What are the barriers to such inclusion?

We can include

Generous, open and inclusive understandings of church best set the platform for evangelization and mission in the contemporary context. I often ask groups with whom I work if they would like to see young people in Church. I invariably get a resounding 'yes', which is often followed by sighs of frustration, anger or futility that betray a certain exasperation or lack of hope. I next make the suggestion that I think that we can include our young in church, but whether we do or not depends more on us than on the youth themselves.

I was once doing some work with the religious education co-ordinator in a Catholic primary school. She told me of her daughter – a young lady who had embraced the spiritual life from a young age. She became involved with Amnesty International and various other humanitarian organizations. She embraced meditation and other ethical ways of living. She volunteered regularly in her local community and was a strong advocate for the disenfranchised.

However, after painting the picture of this beautifully involved and vibrant young woman of whom she was deeply proud, my friend cast her eyes downwards somewhat and added with some sadness:

'... but she doesn't go to Mass.' I reflected how tragic it was that this lady could in any way see herself as a failure after having parented such a beautifully evolved human being who simply chose to live out her response to God in a different way to her mum.

I don't think that we are ever going to see young people (or older ones for that matter) return in their droves to Mass attendance with any great regularity. I'm not saying they shouldn't, I just don't think they will. There are as many sociological factors working against denominational worship in contemporary Australia as there are religious reasons for the decline in practice. Pope Benedict, when he was Cardinal Ratzinger, would seem to hold a similar perspective when, referring to a new 'springtime' for the church, he warned that this future possibility will probably not be about numbers.

Spring time brings new life, hope and possibility. Let us embrace this vision and move forward with confidence. As we pray regularly: let us be spared needless anxiety.

Generosity of vision

The vision for church espoused by Vatican II reflects generosity, openness, dialogue and inclusion. This vision remembers that Jesus was the 'great includer'! How inclusive can we be when it comes to membership of the church? As a parent and Catholic educator, I hope that this spirit of inclusion can extend to the thousands of wonderful young people I have met who may never formally affiliate with a worshipping community. A recent review in the *Tablet* suggests that 'God the Holy Spirit surely speaks to all creation, not just people we judge to have "got it right" religiously. I have talked to too many spiritually alive young people who are without formal religion to believe in that kind of divisiveness.' I'm sure that we can all resonate with this perspective!

Our youth may not relate to church in traditional ways and may insist that the church they choose to belong to is very different from the experience that we have become comfortable with. Our challenge is to be faithful to a living tradition that will at once challenge and dialogue with the culture of our young. At all times we must celebrate and encourage the efforts of our young people to bring about the Kingdom of God in their world.

The cost of exclusion

Poorer Catholic families are almost certainly under-represented in our schools. Recent research tells us that Catholic families on low incomes are twice as likely to be enrolled in a government school as a Catholic school. This is particularly true of secondary students. The *Catholic School in the Third Millennium* document warns that some Catholic schools are unable to fulfil their full potential in the church because they exclude the poor and marginalized on account of their inability to pay fees, 'leading to a selection according to means which deprives the Catholic school of one of its distinguishing features, which is to be a school for all' (par. 7).

Authenticity by inclusion

In church and Catholic education circles around the country, we increasingly hear the question: 'What must we do to maintain our schools as authentically Catholic?' One response to this question has traditionally been to limit the numbers of non-Catholics who can gain entry to the schools so that a 'critical mass' of Catholics can be maintained and thus we can say that we have truly Catholic schools. Percentages vary but most systems around the country have guidelines in this area.

It strikes me as sad that we would have to focus on excluding people in order to maintain our authenticity, when our Gospel says with great clarity that authenticity in Christianity demands inclusion of the marginalized. Authenticity for Catholic schools will not be enhanced by excluding non-Catholics but rather by our inclusion of the poor and those at the margins. Our openness to inclusion and embracing responsibility for 'the other' determines our capacity to be authentically Catholic schools.

The heart of mission

In a letter he sent in 1882 to the Town Clerk of Richmond in Victoria, Br Ambrose Treacy clearly articulated his vision for a Catholic school. Br Treacy said that

> The school is open to all who wish to avail themselves of it without distinction of creed, colour or nationality. No child can be refused admission on the score of religion or of payment.

Clearly, for Br Treacy, inclusion of those at the margins of society is a core value and touchstone for authenticity in our mission. Our mission is always focused on the marginalized. It gives priority to inclusion and an authentic preferential option for the poor. It contends that we cannot fully claim the title 'Catholic' without this emphasis on inclusion and outreach to those on the margins.

Our schools must be founded on the Gospel priorities of inclusion and special concern for young people at risk of being left behind. They must be schools for all who seek the values of our Gospel, regardless of religious affiliation or financial capacity.

Our schools expand the notion of excellence beyond the academic, cultural and sporting domains, as important as they are to holistic education. An excellent Catholic school celebrates success and potential in all domains of the formation of the young. All are nurtured towards fullness of life. Our schools ask hard questions of themselves in terms of how success is defined and how our lived priorities reflect those of the Gospel. School life congruent with our vision is central to our claims of authenticity. This is the tradition to which we belong.

Along with the core priorities of inclusion, service and deep commitment to social justice; advocacy, speaking for the voiceless, should also be a priority. As well as serving those who are at the margins, there is a renewed call to question why people are marginalized and, more importantly, to encourage and give skills to the marginalized in our world to be able to ask these questions for themselves.

Advocacy is surely one of the most sacred tasks of education. We are called to be advocates for those who are marginalized in our world and to teach our young to question the realities they have inherited, since many of these realities are dehumanizing.

We encourage our young to claim the freedom that they have been given in our society. This freedom is not permission to do as we want, but the responsibility to do as we ought for the making of a better world.

Schools for all

Some time ago, I was at one of our schools presenting a Certificate of Accreditation as an Authentic Catholic school in the Edmund Rice tradition as a follow-up to their School Renewal.

I was in the middle of my speech to the college assembly when a young man stood up and began to shout in very strong language his disapproval of what I was saying. His outburst included several four-letter words and it was clear that he was deeply distressed.

In a state of shock, I halted my speech and was deeply moved by what subsequently happened. The first thing I noticed was that the other students did not laugh or react excessively. I next noticed the gentleness of the staff members who moved to calm the young man and attend to his needs. Before much time elapsed, the principal moved to the podium and said something like this:

> This goes to the very heart of our authenticity as a Catholic school. This young man [he named the boy] has special needs and his behaviour is sometimes unacceptable. However, he is a loved member of our community. He has a home in this school and always will have.

I needed to say nothing more to affirm this community as an authentic Catholic school.

Centring the poor

Some time ago, I was with my family at an outdoor restaurant in Lima, Peru. We had just finished the meal and were in the process of paying the bill, when a young girl who had been watching us eat from a distance came and sat on the ground beside our table. With this young girl, who would have been about 19 or 20 years old, was a baby; it could have been her own child, or possibly her little brother or sister.

When you eat in this restaurant, you are served a little bowl of corn as an appetizer – just as in Australia where you may get a bowl of peanuts: very cheap and easy. As we were about to leave the restaurant, the young girl sitting on the ground asked if she could have the leftover bowls of corn that were on our table. To my great shame I found two or three half-empty bowls of corn and handed them down to this young girl, and her baby, to eat.

A couple of minutes later, the girl noticed that some of our softdrink bottles weren't empty, that some of our party had left a little in the bottles. She asked if she could have these bottles so that she could have a drink. This was too much for me, and I asked the waitress to bring a fresh softdrink so that the girl and her child could drink.

We left the restaurant that day, but the image of that young girl haunted me and continues to do so.

I profess to be a Christian, a follower of Jesus, who was the great includer of people. The scandal of Jesus' ministry was that he didn't hand out food or hand down bowls to people – he sat down at the table with them. He invited them to the table! I was deeply ashamed that I'd missed out on that opportunity to invite the young girl to the table. I went back to the restaurant each day at lunchtime – not for the food, but hoping to find that girl and her baby and invite her to the table.

As followers of Jesus we should never be satisfied by giving to the poor from our excess. It is never enough. It is a hallmark of charity, not commitment. Our commitment must be to 'centre' the poor and make our response to their plight the core of our mission. Who we are is determined by those we include!

A 'big' church

On the day of the election of our new pope, Francis, I thought of my dad's relationship with the church when he was alive. He was never a regular Mass attender, although all his life he considered himself a Christian and a Catholic. Dad's way of living out that belonging to church was quite unusual.

Dad personally knew every priest who came to our country town. On the morning of their birthdays, Dad would always turn up at the presbytery with a brand new white shirt from his store and give it to the priest. He could size anyone from a distance and had impeccable taste. Apart from going to Mass at Christmas and Easter and encouraging his kids to go regularly, this was the way in which my dad lived out his place in the Catholic Church.

Our church needs to be a big church – big enough to include the pope, big enough to include my dad, and big enough to include the thousands of young people for whom we care but who may never live out their relationship with the Gospel in traditional Catholic ways.

Our church can be as inclusive as we dare to imagine. When we reflect on what Pope Francis believes, what Edmund Rice believed, what Moses believed, what my dad believed and what I believe, there are probably some very stark differences. However, what makes us all one church is not a sense that everyone must believe everything in the same way. If this were the case, we would not be 'catholic' in the full sense of the word. What makes our church a church of possibility for the future is the fact that all the people I mention, plus the thousands of young people we nurture, belong to a tradition of faith that calls us all to belong and contribute according to our unique gifts and talents.

This vision of church is one that will allow us to continue our mission in Catholic education with great confidence that our young people will make their unique contribution to it. We need to let go of the 'outcomes', but trust that the tradition of faith will be powerful enough, captivating enough and sustaining enough to nurture all the young people we work with as they find their place in the world.

The basics

At one time I worked in the area of state school religious education in the Toowoomba diocese. One of my tasks was to help the catechists who volunteer to go into state schools to teach religious education. This is real mission stuff! Most of the students in the Catholic classes for religious education were not churched in any formal sense of the word. Those who did not opt out of religious education were put into classes according to the denomination mentioned in their enrolment form.

On one occasion, I received a phone call from a lady in the west of Queensland asking for advice, as the students in her class were very unreceptive. I asked what she was teaching in her class and she responded that she was only teaching 'the basics'. As will become evident, the basics for that wonderful lady might not have been the basics that these students needed to hear.

Three weeks later, at the request of this lady, I went to visit her class. I walked into the classroom, where waiting was a group of mixed Year 9/10 students, on a hot summer's day in a very small confined space. The lady began her class. The topic for the lesson was the Sorrowful Mysteries of the Rosary. I am not saying that there is no place for the Sorrowful Mysteries of the Rosary in a catechetical religious education program. What's more, I would never dare question the centrality of these beliefs and practices to the faith of this wonderful catechist who in her way of thinking was only teaching kids 'the basics'.

The basics for a person who is a 'womb to tomb' Catholic of Irish stock may include a strong emphasis on Catholic cultural practices such as the Rosary. However, these un-churched children needed to hear a different version of 'the basics'. They needed first of all to hear about Jesus Christ. They needed to hear his Gospel and the central message of his life. They needed to look at the potential that this Gospel could have for enhancing their lives. Whether or not any of them would ever get around to incorporating the Sorrowful Mysteries of the Rosary in their spirituality is doubtful. What I found I had to say to this lady was that if she continued to teach her version of the basics – that is, to presume a readiness on the part of the students that was just not there – she was going to continue to have problems and be unsuccessful.

This was the stuff of ongoing conversations, not only with this lady but with all those engaged in this difficult task.

The extra step

As we become immersed in the busyness of our year, let us take the time to remind one another of the privilege that is ours in Catholic education. The insights into authenticity presented by EREA's Charter and its Touchstones challenge us always to go the extra step in our service of the Gospel and its priorities. Inclusion of those at the margins of our society is at the core of the Gospel.

Some time ago I had a conversation with a friend of mine, the principal of a Catholic high school in the developing world. This school has enjoyed considerable success in recent years and has become the school of choice for families in its city who can afford to pay the fees. Sadly, this success and increased demand has driven up fees and the poor, who once had more ready access to the school, now find it very expensive.

Disturbed by this trend, the principal decided that the school would offer a separate shift in the afternoons, where students from humble and poorer backgrounds could attend. They enjoy a similar quality of education as those who pay full fees and who study in the morning, but they pay much less. This is a genuine attempt to respond to the reality of that society in a Gospel-centred way; and we should applaud this desire to include the marginalized. However, could the power of this response be strengthened by adding an extra step in the process of enrolment?

The kids who attend in the afternoons know that they are poor. They don't need another level of labelling to contribute to their awareness of where they fit into society. By attending in the afternoon, their place in the world is confirmed for them and for all who know them and the school. Why not could the names of all who are accepted to study at this school be put into a ballot where names are randomly selected for study in either mornings or afternoons? The parents who can afford to pay may be confronted by and resistant to this, but is it not the stuff of the Gospel? Segregation has never advanced the good of a society or the formation of individuals within that society.

The Gospel challenges us to include an extra step similar to this. Catholic schools must always resist the challenge of elitism:

the temptation simply to accommodate the poor rather than give them an equal place at the table. This may require us to be counter-cultural and out of step with society's norms – the way things are traditionally done.

The challenge of inclusion

Let us aspire to a vision for Catholic education in which parents, fully informed from the point of original interview, accept that part of their school fee dollar goes towards the support of needy families inside and outside their school community. This would be a source of great pride. You might say that this indirectly happens now with grant redistribution processes and fee relief in schools. However, let us make this a known consequence of what a Catholic school does, an essential part of who we are and what we believe: a springboard to evangelization of our communities into a deeper sense of what the Gospel demands of us.

Are we bold enough to review scales of fees in our schools so that people pay according to their possibility, so that all who seek the core values we offer feel welcome to apply without fear of a loss of dignity? My experience is that efforts in this direction bring out the best and worst in human nature. I was once part of an effort to offer holders of Commonwealth Health Care Cards reduced fees in Catholic schools. Sadly, many parents of already enrolled students objected strongly that these people were 'sponging' off them as full fee payers and would bring problems into the schools, since it was perceived that the poor are 'problematic'. Clearly, we have much work to do!

These attitudes become the field for challenge and evangelization. Yes, we all know that our tax system allows people to minimalize income and misrepresent their reality. But should this minority dissuade us from exploring the possibility? As Chesterton once said, 'The Christian ideal has not been tried and found wanting. It has been found difficult, and left untried!'

TOUCHSTONE 4

Education promoting justice and solidarity

'The only question we will have to answer at the end of time is how we have treated the poor.'
   (Bishop Samuel Ruiz Garcia of Mexico)

Catholic education must make bold claims about humanity and the way in which human beings should engage in our world. We speak for the voiceless and those who are excluded. Bold statements must also be made about the future of our world, about justice, about the way in which we are expected to relate to one another, about the dignity of every human life. We don't pretend that it is possible to envisage a Christianity that is divorced from these issues. A middle class, non-engaged Christianity doesn't make sense; it's a contradiction in terms! If we recover anything of the message and priorities of Jesus, we must understand that this is what he fought against. Injustice and exclusion in the status quo was never acceptable to Jesus.

No poor – no Gospel

We fool ourselves if we think we can witness to the vision of Jesus or do Catholic education, without a clear option for those who are marginalized and excluded. Catholic schools in our Australian culture are on the precipice: we can either fulfil our mission to be counter-cultural, inclusive and embracing of a genuine option for the poor or have this remembered in the future as our omission.

A church that does not stand with the poor betrays the vision of Jesus who was a poor person and identified with those who were poor and at the margins of his world. Dom Pedro Casaldaliga of Brazil is most insistent: 'We must keep repeating it: without the poor there is no salvation, without the poor there is no church, without the poor there is no Gospel.'

An inclusive, large God

In reality, neither the church nor Catholic education really has a mission – the mission has *us*! We believe in a God who offers the fullness of life and fullness of love and compassion to all of humanity: an inclusive, large God! The outpouring from God to the world – that is the mission! Our privilege is to participate in this mission that precedes us all because of the nature of our God.

Our embodiment of this mission requires that we align our priorities with God's priorities as they are stated in the Gospel and stand in solidarity with those who are 'blessed' in the eyes of our God – the peacemakers, the merciful, those who thirst for justice, as well as, the poor, the powerless, the excluded, the marginalized, the humble, and the suffering.

For the sake of the Kingdom

I suggest that there is no room for a tame and meek Jesus. The Jesus we present must be the Jesus who said 'yes' in the garden of Gethsemane, who decided to stay for the sake of the Reign of God, who saw what was wrong in his culture and fought to bring about change in people's hearts. In our quest to engage the spiritual imagination of the young, let us introduce them to a Jesus who offered fullness of life for women, for lepers, and who repeatedly questioned authority in the interests of the Reign of God.

Let us also introduce our young to Mary as she is portrayed in the *Magnificat*, that prayer of solidarity with the poor, social justice and liberation. Mary rejoices in the God who shows special regard for the poor and marginalized. This prayer does not portray Mary as a shy, silent comforter of the disturbed, but rather the disturber of the comfortable. What a magnificent image of leadership for the Reign of God!

Shalom

The Reign of God that Jesus proclaimed ushered in a new world order characterized by relationships based on justice, love and peace. The Hebrew word for peace is *shalom*. *Shalom* refers not so much to an absence of violence but to a 'right order' — to health, prosperity, security, to political and spiritual wellbeing. It implies a sense of equity and fairness in our dealings with each other. There is no *shalom* if children go hungry, if human rights are ignored; there is no *shalom* in a world indifferent to the common good.

The core questions

My formation to this point has led me to believe that the most important questions that anyone who undertakes ministry in the light of the Gospel must address are: Who are the poor and the excluded in my world? What does the liberation promised by the Christian Gospel mean for the people I minister to?

The absolute centrality of these questions to discussion about Christian mission was highlighted for me some years ago when I went with a friend to Sri Lanka to meet up with theologian Fr Tissa Balasuriya. Fr Tissa was once formally excommunicated from the church because of some of his writings. He was subsequently admitted back but the whole incident caused Fr Tissa enormous personal hardship and divided the Sri Lankan church.

'So you've come to talk theology!' Fr Tissa said when we first met. He promptly led us out of the room, down the stairs, across the compound, into the street, into a rickshaw, and before we fully realized what was happening, we had travelled for 45 minutes to the outskirts of Colombo to a slum area where he had built a school. He took us to an area on the unfinished roof of the school, right in the middle of the slum, sat us down and said: '*Now* we can do theology. We *cannot* do theology out of the context of the poor and what the Gospel means for them!'

Fr Tissa was implying that to speak of the Reign of God without focusing on the poor is impossible. Christianity is not possible unless the poor are at its centre. As Joan Chittister argues: 'To say that we believe that God loves the poor, judges on their behalf, wills their deliverance but do nothing ourselves to free the poor, to hear their pleas, to lift their burdens, to act in their behalf, is an empty faith indeed.' Ignoring the poor means that we ignore God, since through our attempts to overcome poverty and marginalization we participate in God's plan. Quite simply, it is the way of Jesus' disciples.

Receiving an education, not gaining a qualification

I remember sitting on the roof of Loreto Day School Sealdah, a very prestigious and highly esteemed girls school in Kolkata. The most authentically Catholic school I know. Ironically, there are very few

Catholics enrolled. What a study of inclusion! If you are looking for inspiration as a leader in Catholic education try to visit this place. If you can't visit, at least Google Sr Cyril Mooney, the dynamic and charismatic principal who refers to her school as a 'resource centre for the poor'.

For generations this prestigious school has been the school of choice for many of the well-heeled people of Kolkata, regardless of their religious affiliation. Under Sr Cyril, of the school's enrolment of 1500 half pay high fees and half pay nothing. This latter group are street kids, the poorest of the poor. All wear school uniforms and all are equal in this remarkable place. But that's not all! All the children — whether they are well-to-do, the future leaders of India, or children of street sweepers — every day are asked to teach other street kids — kids from the villages and railway stations, kids who have nothing. It is compulsory, regardless of caste or family background.

I remember asking a very eloquent school leader — a high-caste young lady of about 15 years of age, why her dad, who could afford any type of education, would send her to Loreto Sealdah, a school where she had to engage with people of a caste and a family background very different from her own. She replied very eloquently, and I think this is something we can all take note of. She said, 'My father sends me to this school so that I can receive an education, not just attain a qualification!' An *education* for that young girl, who was not a Christian by the way, means engagement with the 'other' and the use of our gifts in service to the marginalized.

Some might be tempted to say that it is easier for a school in India or the developing world to embrace an option for the poor, as poverty is all around. However, as Mother Teresa once said, 'Kolkata can be seen all over the world if you only have eyes to see!'

The uncomfortable truth

Before the Second Vatican Council, the catch-phrase 'Outside the church, there is no salvation!' motivated the church's attempts at evangelization. However, liberation theologians suggest another take on the priorities of Jesus when they coined the term 'Outside the poor, there is no salvation!' Authentic conversion of the church, its members and its structures, takes place through solidarity with the outcasts of the world.

At times this can become an uncomfortable discussion for us in the Western world. It centres on the materially poor and by most measures we are not poor; it may challenge existing structures and on many of those structures we may have built our careers and community life. Let us enter this discussion on a journey towards greater authenticity and be heartened by the words of Gustavo Gutierrez when he says that 'Any time privileged people come to know poor people, it is a good thing!'

Keeping us on the hook

There is a temptation in our Western church to spiritualize poverty; that is, to speak solely of the 'spiritually' poor, which would probably include most of us in some way or another. It is clear that Catholic education has a mission to those in our society who suffer cultural oppression, have lost direction spiritually or who are searching for meaning in the context of a society dominated by rampant consumerism and secular gods and idols. However, these definitions of poverty cannot be used to let us off the hook when it comes to the Gospel imperative to serve the materially poor — those whose dignity as human beings is affronted by marginalization and lack of opportunity and choice. As Congregation Leader of the Christian Brothers, Philip Pinto, says, these are the people who suffer all forms of poverty!

The materially poor are those for whom life itself is a heavy burden. They have no voice, no dignity; many have no name, no recognized existence. They lack adequate educational and healthcare opportunities and are excluded from decisions that affect them. The poor are those who do not take life for granted, those for whom staying alive is their primary task and many die before their time. Liberation theologians would suggest that these are the 'non-persons': they are the voiceless, the silent ones of history, the poorest of the poor.

With and for the poor

The term 'preferential option for the poor' is commonly used these days in mission statements and the like. In Spanish, the verb *optar* implies making a significant decision according to one's deepest values and priorities. The use of this verb implies much more than a simple choice between alternatives. For us, the use of the term should refer to a fundamental orientation in our lives and our structures towards the plight of the poor – their needs and concerns.

When liberation theologians use the term 'preferential option for the poor', they are inferring that God makes a decision to stand with and for the poor. God loves the poor. He loves them preferentially but not exclusively. 'The last will be the first and the first will be last.' The rich will be there – but they will be last.

The preference is not because the poor are good, but because God is good. As Gutierrez says, 'God has a preferential love for the poor not because they are necessarily better than others, morally or religiously, but simply because they are poor, and living in an inhuman situation is contrary to God's will.'

The key question for a genuine option for the poor is: How do I tell the excluded that God loves them and that the Gospel is good news?

Mission or omission

At the end of the first session of the Second Vatican Council, Cardinal Vaccaro lamented that 'Something has been missing so far in the Council', and he asked, 'Where shall we find that vital impulse, that soul, that fullness of spirit?' He replied, 'This is the hour of the poor, of the millions of poor who are everywhere on the earth.'

In coming to this conclusion, perhaps the Cardinal reflected on Gandhi's suggestion that whenever we are in doubt and unsure what to do, we must recall the face of the poorest and weakest person we have seen and ask whether or not the action we are contemplating will restore life and dignity to that person. The path forward then becomes clear.

Should we in Catholic education ask ourselves a similar question to that proposed by the good Cardinal? Will an option for the poor in Catholic education be our mission, or perhaps will it remain an omission! The Gospel we serve clearly directs our mission to the margins, to the disadvantaged, to those who lack hope. Compassionate engagement with the world is indispensible to the way in which Christians worship a loving God who stands with and for the poor.

Leaving security

I have been very fortunate to visit India on many occasions. In India, one is clearly able to observe the importance of water and rivers in the spiritual psyche of the people. In ancient times, rivers not only held religious and ritual significance but often served as boundaries between princely states and regions. To cross a river was often a movement into the unknown, into a new country.

I am always deeply moved by the story of the Buddha's initial leaving of his father's kingdom and moving out into the unknown world, from which he had always been protected. One of the first things that he had to do in his journey to salvation was cross a river that separated his father's kingdom, a place of of surety and comfort, from the wider world which was full of uncertainty, lack of security and potentially much misery.

It can be argued that crossing the river was the most important moment in the Buddha's life. It heralded the beginning of his new life alongside the poor majority in his world. Crossing the river marked the first significant moment in the Buddha's mission to free his world from greed, hate and delusion.

Crossing the river

One of my favourite movies is *The Motorcycle Diaries*. This movie tells the true story of the revolutionary Ernesto (Che) Guevara's early life. The young Ernesto, recently finished his medical degree, travelled with a friend around Latin America on an old motorbike. During the course of his travels, he grew into a deep appreciation of the plight of the poor of Latin America at that time who were victims of structural injustice. The movie is a study in change and conversion.

My favourite scene in the movie is when Ernesto is celebrating his birthday with priests and nuns in a leper colony on the banks of the Amazon in Peru. As a medical doctor, he specialized in the treatment of tropical diseases. The place where the lepers live is an island in the middle of the very wide river, separated from the world.

At one point Ernesto goes outside and looks towards the island. In a moment of decision, he dives into the river and swims towards the lepers. On the riverbank his friends call him back because it is dangerous and he suffers from chronic asthma. On the shore of the island, however, the lepers encourage him to continue swimming towards them.

This is a wonderful image of conversion; of movement towards 'the other', of letting go of the self and of baptism into solidarity with the poor. Ernesto reached the island and his life was never to be the same. He had chosen his option: he has swum the river – he is with the poor. In much of his later life, Ernesto was not a role model that we would necessarily follow. However, I think that all Christians at some point in their life need to work out on what side of the river they are going to stand when it comes to embracing an option for the poor.

Voice of the 'non-person'

The women I am about to refer to would not see themselves as inspirational or leaders in any traditional sense. I encountered these three women recently in India. They are all desperately poor and uneducated and yet the stark simplicity of what they taught me remains with me and continues to inspire me in ways that people with titles seldom can. My hope is that these remarkable people will also be a source of inspiration for you.

The first of these women belongs to a self-help group – a group of women who come together for mutual support and projects of micro finance and discussion of women's issues in a rural village. Our partners in Delhi organized a meeting of the group with the 13 travellers from Edmund Rice Education who were visiting the village.

In our meeting, one question put to the women was: 'What difference has belonging to this group and receiving education in these basic things made to you in your life and the life of your family?' One of them, a Muslim, unused to speaking in public, particularly with male strangers, put up her hand and said, 'Before I joined the self-help group, I had no voice, but now I can speak!' This simple woman reminded me of the central role of education in giving people a voice to speak – education is liberation and a way forward for those at the margins.

The second woman is probably not with us any more. When I met her, she was lying in an AIDS hospital outside the city of

Hyderabad, very close to death. Our group was touring the hospital, interacting with many of the patients, but this lady was far too weak to engage. She was young and we were told she had young children. I remember observing her lying on her cot, with the look on her face of someone who was about to die.

I was the last to leave the room. On my way out, I offered this lady a sign of peace – '*Namaste*'. To my total surprise, her face lit up; she found strength that I didn't think she had and responded with her own '*Namaste*' and made an unsuccessful effort to get up. The effort she made through her suffering humbled me to the core. It reminded me that I should never ignore anyone; that no one should be left behind; that education should be inclusive of and full of respect for all, whatever the cost.

The third was a young woman working with a group of girls in domestic labour in the city of Kolkata. One of our partner groups was organizing these girls into a something akin to a union or a collective so that basic human rights could be advocated for and that they might have a voice. Our partners go along to the employers of these girls to make sure some basic rights are in place – perhaps a day off a week, perhaps time to visit family occasionally and some justice in wages and conditions.

When this girl first went to a gathering, she was handed an identification card, a card that had her name on it. Even though she could not read or write, she had been taught to recognize her name in writing. When she was handed the card she burst into tears.

Asked why she was crying, she replied that when she received the name card it was the first time in her whole life that she been formally recognized as a human being, as having an identity. It was the first time that she had been given the sense that she was someone. Previously, she had been a 'non-person'.

This concept of the non-person is something that is quite foreign to us in the West. A non-person is someone who has no rights, someone who is not even registered as being alive, someone who would normally live and die without any identity. When theologians talk about the 'non-person', they are talking about the voiceless, the silent ones of history, the poorest of the poor. In the light of this reality, Gustavo Gutierrez proposes that Christian mission must focus on 'how to tell the non-person that God is love, and that this love makes us all brothers and sisters.'

The movement to confer on that young girl a sense of identity, as someone who is known, loved and valued, is a powerful indicator of what all education must do. I thank that young girl for inspiring me, as a Christian and an educator, not to forget the voiceless, not to forget the 'non-persons'.

Co-responsibility: our way of being in relationship

Part of the levy paid by member schools of Edmund Rice Education Australia is used in a process of support for special works and schools struggling for one reason or another given the name 'co-responsibility'.

As Pope John XXIII once said, 'We are not on earth to guard a museum, but to cultivate a flourishing garden of life.' In our attempts to embrace an option for the poor into the future, I don't think the answer is to dismantle our well-off schools and focus solely on 'alternative' education. It would be a sad reality indeed if this was our only response in our quest for greater authenticity. Flexible learning centres and annexes cannot be the entirety of our combined efforts to embrace an option for the materially poor!

Edmund Rice Education tries to model a family of schools where those who can look after those who can't, where co-responsibility becomes the norm, where the strong accept responsibility for those on the margins.

Co-responsibility means much more than just giving money —as important as this is. Co-responsibility is a win-win situation. There aren't donors and receivers — we all give and we all receive. We contribute according to our possibilities and we receive according to our need. We are all liberated through our participation in the liberation of the weakest. The poor enrich us and complete our humanity.

Co-responsibility is a way of being in relationship. It is based on an appreciation that the whole is as strong as its parts, that this national family called EREA requires that we cast our lots together, that the strong will always assist those who are struggling and that we are all winners through the experience of this relationship.

Bringing co-responsibility from the stage of being a mechanism for supporting struggling schools and programs such as Youth Plus to a deeply held appreciation of our unique way of being in relationship is a clear priority for our future.

The power of immersion

> *We returned to our places, these Kingdoms,*
> *But no longer at ease here, in the old dispensation,*
> *With an alien people clutching their gods.*
>
> T. S. Eliot, *The Journey of the Magi*

Why do we put so much energy and resources into cross-cultural immersion experiences for our students and staff?

To be involved in an immersion is to engage in what is called 'deep travel'. The traveller steps out of the ordinary into active anticipation, into encountering difference, and welcomes moments that broaden and deepen an appreciation of the world. Economist Miriam Beard echoed this when she remarked that 'travel is more than seeing of sites; it is a change that goes on deep and permanent in one's ideas on living.' Travel is, at its best, a transformative encounter with difference. In political and theological terms; it is an encounter with 'the other'.

Just as authentic inter-religious dialogue can only happen when there is true openness to conversion through accepting the God-experience of the other, immersion is most successful when the life experience of the other calls values into question and provokes deep reflection on the lifestyle and choices of the participant.

On a practical level, the act of departing the known and physically leaving home is a ritual that prepares an individual for an experience that is difficult to orchestrate at home. The physical discipline of undertaking the journey is preparation for the encounter to come. The journey suspends the demands of daily life, opening us up to new possibilities. Leaving the everyday allows us to change the lens and adjust the filter.

The intention of an immersion experience is not just to encounter a foreign culture. In our context, it is to encounter the world of the poor — which is the world of the majority. These experiences bring an individual into direct contact with this majority world: the dollar-a-day world, the world where women walk miles to harvest water and children walk even further for schooling, where low-caste men are beaten for drawing water from a pond, where life expectancy is determined by the colour of one's skin, where dowry deaths are common and where Western businesses promote dangerous products long after they are banned at home. A purposeful immersion allows the traveller to put flesh and blood, real faces, real names to the conversation about social justice that so often happens at home in safe settings.

In educational terms, an immersion can be the beginning of the slow process of conscientisation, the first step in both personal and political change. Immersion forces questions to the surface – how can this be so? The experience allows a traveller to return home and to look at his or her own circumstance with greater clarity. Immersion has led many to a profound review of life, to a commitment to live more simply, to commit to the poor, not just in theory but by becoming increasingly involved to champion the cause. To paraphrase a theme that Philip Pinto often speaks of, immersion can be a vehicle for 'subversion'.

However, like all education, an immersion works within the limits of those who participate. Some will take much from the experience and the change will be profound and immediate; others may take a little and change may surface many years on. But the commitment by our schools to this regular discipline of encounter with the majority world remains, at its core, a profound act of evangelization and a defining Christian act.

Go with an open heart and be surprised.

The 'poop' of life

Presence, liberation and compassion are celebrated by the Christian Brothers and those who work with them as core pillars of the philosophy and ministry of Edmund Rice. I personally have never had any problem in understanding the centrality of liberation and compassion, but have struggled somewhat with the notion of 'presence'. Just recently, I had an experience that shed light for me on the importance of being present to the reality of others.

During the 2014 General Chapter of the Christian Brothers in the Kenyan capital of Nairobi, I went on an immersion experience to Kibera, the largest urban slum in Africa. Towards the end of an extraordinary day, one of our guides invited us to go to her home to meet her family. The house was very humble, basically a tin shed, but the time spent with this family was very special.

Attached to the house was another little shed where the family cared for orphaned babies from the slum. When the lady who was caring for the kids came to greet my companions and me, a little baby girl, left alone, began to cry. I went over and picked the little girl up and she looked into my eyes and stopped crying. However, what happened next taught me an extraordinary lesson.

Our little group had been very compliant with the suggestion given before the immersion day not to bring cameras. We discussed the difference between being 'tourists' and being 'pilgrims' during this experience. When I picked the little girl up and received a beautiful smile in return, I immediately thought that this would have been a great photo opportunity. No sooner had the thought entered my mind, however, than the little girl 'pooped' all over me! Yellow and runny, full measure!

While I was looking for a photo opportunity, annoyed that no one had a camera, the little girl told me in the most basic of ways that she was a human being in need of my care and attention. What a profound way to be reminded that I was not a tourist in Kibera, consuming an experience, but a pilgrim there to share our common humanity.

As I cleaned myself up, I reminded myself that the core focus of Jesus' ministry was the offer of fullness of life to all through the sharing of common humanity. His 'curriculum' was life and his 'methodology' was inclusion of all. He was about life and, in any single moment, about a life — that of the person in front of him who needed to know that this abundance of life is offered to all.

I give thanks for this little girl and her stark reminder of these truths, although I hope it won't need reminding in that particular way any time soon!

Authentic worship

Recently, I had the great privilege of spending time with the Christian Brothers' community on the island of Negros in the Philippines. In this community, three Australian brothers work hard in their different outreaches in education and do wonderful work for the poor in the footsteps of Edmund Rice.

One evening during our visit, a colleague and I were asked by the brothers to lead the community in evening prayer. We put considerable time into preparing this prayer experience and planned each step carefully so that the prayer could run as smoothly as possible.

However, in the middle of the prayer time, at a reflective stage, there was an interruption. One of the brothers left the chapel and returned a couple of minutes later with a family of mother, father and a little baby, together with a lady who worked closely with the brothers.

I must admit that my first reaction was one of annoyance that this reflective experience we had worked hard to orchestrate was being interrupted. Why couldn't this family have waited outside until we were finished?

At the end of our prayer time, I heard the full story and was ashamed of my reaction. The little girl, Sophia, was three years old and had recently undergone an operation to remove a tumour from her stomach. When I got a close look at little Sophia, I could see the reason the family had returned that evening – the tumour had emerged again and on her small frame her stomach was as if she had a basketball inside it. Clearly, desperation had brought them to the brothers' house that evening.

Her mum and dad were very poor and they had eight other children and lived some hours away. The brothers had supported the family through Sophia's illness and provided the resources for the initial operation. They had also undertaken to support the family during the potentially expensive subsequent therapies that little Sophia would need. However, it appeared that things were much more dire than originally thought and Sophia was gravely ill.

What did I learn that evening? Upon reflection, I am sure that without doubt, the most pleasing thing to God that happened in that chapel that evening was not our eloquent and well-planned prayers, but the openness of the brothers' community to receive the poor family and to serve them as best they could.

We worship a God who sides with the poor and those at the margins of life. We authentically worship this God by serving and doing all we can for others. Service is worship! It doesn't matter how eloquent and how wonderful our planned prayers and liturgies might be – without a commitment to serve, our worship will always be empty.

As a postscript, the brothers informed me that young Sophia died peacefully some time later, surrounded by her family and those who loved her. I will never forget the little angel who interrupted our prayer that evening. She taught me an invaluable lesson. She taught me that service of and care for those in need is the most complete way we can worship our God.

The church we serve

Edmund Rice Education is a work of and for our church – a church described by our new pope as 'of and for the poor':

- a generous and inclusive church that shows deep love for the poor and marginalized;

- a church that strives to usher in the Reign of God: the promise of fullness of life and true freedom for all in our troubled world;
- a church that proclaims inclusion to be at the heart of the Gospel and exclusion in its many forms its greatest betrayal;
- a church that knows that a school's capacity to make a difference is not simply dependent on its physical resources but on humble resolve within the community to build the Reign of God and embrace solidarity with the excluded ones.

The Charter for Edmund Rice Education and the foundations upon which we stand clearly direct us to the 'margins', to the disadvantaged, to those who lack hope. The church we serve promotes inclusion, service and compassionate engagement with the world as indispensible to the way Christians worship a loving and expansive God.

Leadership and witness
Thoughts for educators

*'She makes me a bad Marxist since she makes
me believe in godliness!'*
*(Indian Communist leader Jyoti Basu speaking
of Mother Teresa)*

The unlived life

Our example is so important. As a parent and an educator, I am continually challenged by the words of Carl Jung. He said: 'Nothing has a stronger influence psychologically on their children than the unlived life of their parents.'

We touch the future by the quality of guidance and formation we give to emerging generations. The ultimate exam we adults face is to live in a future created by our own children. The kind of world they commit themselves to will arise in no small part from the quality of our example.

Inspiration

Isn't leadership all about inspiration? As John Quincy Adams once said, 'If your actions inspire others to dream more, learn more, do more and become more, you are a leader.' Sometimes we are blessed with a podium and words with which to inspire, but mostly what is required are humble witness and selfless example. The irony is that we inspire more through authenticity and humility than by dazzling skills and eloquence.

The quality of our leadership in Catholic education will be measured by our willingness and capacity to inspire and excite, to engage and enlist others in a mission that essentially emanates from our God and our God's loving desire to offer salvation to the whole of humanity.

Influence and the dream

Find out who you are and what you stand for! Have a vision! Dream the dream! Martin Luther King's famous words from his address at the Lincoln Memorial in 1963 struck a chord with the whole world: 'I have a dream!' Note that he didn't say 'I have a strategic plan!' Strategic plans are important but true leaders must be able to dream and inspire others.

The key to successful leadership is influence over others, not title or authority. The shallowest form of leadership relies on titles to assert authority and influence. In her own inimitable way Margaret Thatcher once said words like: 'Being a leader is like being a lady. If you have to tell someone that you are one, you probably aren't!'

I think we get the truth she was pointing out. If leaders have to rely on titles or external endorsement in the hope of gaining respect and support, then they aren't really leaders and they won't inspire.

Jesus said very little about leadership, except to condemn those who misused their position in society for the purposes of personal gain. Rather than talk about it, Jesus modelled leadership. His leadership came from service. All leadership in the Christian context needs to be focused on service. As Christians we are identified and recognized by the quality of our service.

Teach the questions

Those involved in ministry place their search for God and meaning at the disposal of those who wish to join that search but maybe don't know how. We must be prepared to lead our young down new paths, since many of the old have become unhelpful, even toxic. We need to prepare them to speak for the poor and excluded, lest the inhuman cycle continues for another generation. We need to teach them to question and critique our world, not simply inhabit it. As Joan Chittister reminds us, 'It's not the answers we teach them to give, but rather it's the moral questions we teach them to ask, that are the measure of the spiritual leadership we give to the emerging generation.'

My life – my message

The contribution of all staff in Catholic schools – leaders, teachers and those who provide support – should be seen as essential in the education and formation of our students. We contribute by the way we serve in our varying roles but also by the quality of our example and witness to the values of the Christian Gospel.

We all have probably heard lines such as, 'No one can give to others that which they do not themselves possess' and 'Your students will remember more about you than about the material you tried to teach them'. There is a lot of truth in these statements.

We may have wonderful RE programs and Masters degrees in religion but how can we seriously expect to interest our students in the spiritual life if we do not model adult lives that are openly prayerful, searching and God-centred? Marshall McLuhan said many years ago that often in communication 'the medium is the message'. This is an important reminder for us. As a staff member in a Catholic school I am the medium and the witness I give is the message. I think that it is OK to be more than a little frightened by the implications of these thoughts.

I am not suggesting that we all need to be religious fanatics, teach the subject called 'RE' or all be Catholic or think about religion in the same way. But I am proposing that all staff in Catholic schools should give public witness to the truth that spiritual values and a relationship with God are important and worthy of our utmost effort as human beings. Most young people won't identify with us in the role of RE or Science teacher, but they can and will identify with and be touched by wholesome, spiritual, integrated human beings.

Jung was so right when he said:

> An understanding heart is everything in a teacher, and cannot be esteemed highly enough. One looks back with appreciation to the brilliant teachers, but with gratitude to those who touched our human feeling. The curriculum is so much necessary raw material, but warmth is the vital element for the growing plant and for the soul of the child.

The essential ordinary

In many ways teaching is an ordinary job. It is ordinary in the same way that air is ordinary, that water and earth are ordinary, that friendship is ordinary. Teaching is ordinary like parenting is ordinary, like farming is ordinary, like policing and firefighting and driving an ambulance are ordinary. Teachers are public servants. If we were looking for the high life we backed the wrong horse! Teachers work for a wage not for profit; we enjoy little celebrity.

Our job is common – but it is essential, one of society's necessary tasks. It is common – but of the utmost importance. We spend our lives in the company of children, yet we have the most serious of responsibilities. Lee Iacocca, CEO in the 1970s of Ford, then of one of the world's largest corporations, put it this way:

> In a completely rational society, the best of us would aspire to be teachers and the rest of us would have to settle for something less, because passing civilization along from one generation to the next ought to be the highest honour and highest responsibility anyone could have.

What does this responsibility entail? What is expected of us? What is the one great essential task of teaching? Might I suggest that it is simply to believe in the young and through them to believe in the future! Irrespective of what we teach, this is the task.

Often distracted by the demands of the present, we should remind ourselves that the future, tomorrow, is in fact our canvas. As educator Michael Elphick reminds us, the ultimate exam we face is to live in a future created by our own children. What kind of world they commit themselves to will arise in no small part from the quality and tenor of our example.

For the love of it

In recent times we have seen the advent of the new Institutes of Teachers. All states have their own version, a movement towards professional accreditation for teachers. Most are supportive of this new endeavour. We see it as an opportunity to revise our professional standards, to show the wider world that we take seriously the responsibility entrusted to us. The Institute is an initiative that promotes transparency and accountability — values that all can support.

It would be a pity, though, if in our new-found professionalism we lost something of the original notion of what it means to be 'amateur'. In recent years the word has come to be identified with all those things we hope we are not — clumsy, inefficient and unprofessional. The term 'amateur' comes from the Latin term that means 'to love'. So in its original form the term simply means someone who 'does it for love', who seeks not fame or fortune but rather the simple pleasure of the task itself. In this sense of the word, then, I hope those of us who give ourselves to ministry in Catholic schools can be described as true 'amateurs'.

The greatest teachers I have encountered are those who have

embraced teaching as a calling, a vocation. And I don't mean this in any mystical or metaphysical sense. I am simply suggesting that the great teachers among us see their daily round not simply as a job but as the way in which their lives contribute to the great vocation that God calls us all to, the building of God's Kingdom.

To help the young find purpose and meaning – be it through the formal study of religion, the sciences or the humanities, or through pastoral care in our schools – this is our task. Teaching is essentially a religious activity. In education, we aim to lead students to discover in an ever-deepening way their giftedness and uniqueness, to develop and celebrate this uniqueness and then to offer it for the common good.

Michael Elphick suggests that it is this sense of loving service that the Thomas More character had in mind in Robert Bolt's famous play *A Man for All Seasons*. Early in the play, More attempts to divert Richard Rich, an ambitious man who sought worldly fame and recognition, from political ambition into teaching:

More says to Rich, 'Why not be a teacher? You'd be a fine teacher; perhaps a great one.' Rich counters with, 'If I was, who would know it?' Moore responds, 'You; your pupils; your friends; God. Not a bad public, that. Become a teacher!'

Let us all commit to the notion of teaching as ministry, as calling. Let us commit to professionalism, to be sure, but at the same time let us recognize our true status as amateurs. Let us take up More's challenge to be good teachers, perhaps even great ones!

Restoring the balance

I recently came across a photo of a stand of trees on King Island which have grown leaning heavily to one side; it is clear that over the course of time the trees' growth has become permanently distorted by the prevailing winds on the island. Lack of balance appears normal.

Similarly, some would say that the central priorities for education in this country have been distorted in recent times by an over-preoccupation in public debate and government policy on class sizes, standardised testing and simplistically measurable outcomes. This was the argument offered recently in a *Four Corners* program that highlighted the development and change that had happened in three separate and very different schools throughout Australia.

The central message of the program was that these schools had become successful primarily because there had been a renewed emphasis on the relationship between teachers and students; priority was given to leadership for teaching and learning based on these relationships; and high expectations in learning and behaviour had been put before the young people and they had responded appropriately.

I have the sense that Catholic educators have always instinctively been aware of this truth. We contribute by the way we serve in our varying roles but we also know the importance of the quality of our example and witness to the values of the Christian Gospel.

Mahatma Gandhi once said in a famous quote that 'My life is my message.' Should anyone settle for less? Anyone in education should understand that who they are, what they stand for and how they live their lives is the most important message that young people receive. How can we seriously expect to interest our students in learning and the spiritual life if we do not model to them adult lives that are openly prayerful, searching and God-centred? All staff in Catholic schools give witness to the truth that spiritual values and a relationship with God are important and worthy of our utmost effort as human beings.

The only agenda

Christian leaders bring about change by drawing those they serve into a deeper sense of their core values and what the Gospel asks of them. I recently saw the movie *Invictus*, which, as well as telling the story of South Africa's 1992 World Cup Rugby win, deals with the life of Nelson Mandela after his release from prison and his early time as president. There were many messages that came through in this story: strong themes of forgiveness and reconciliation and the extraordinary capacity of a human being to put the past behind and look to the future.

One of the most poignant lessons for me was the way in which Nelson Mandela dealt with the rugby establishment of South Africa, which in many ways epitomized the apartheid regime of the time. As newly elected President, Mandela could have brought down the rugby establishment and had much support to do this from within his own community. After all, people had suffered for a long time at the hands of apartheid, and the 'white' world of rugby in the country at the time typified this era.

What Mandela did, though, was not bring rugby down. Instead, he worked with those involved in the establishment – not to make them feel horrible about things in the past, but to think more deeply about what was intrinsically good for the future of the country. He challenged those of privilege to rediscover their depth of values so that they could in turn, through their success, influence the success of his emerging nation. It was an extraordinary story of Mandela's capacity to put behind him the need for retribution and to work positively towards galvanising support for the future of his fledgling nation. In this type of leadership the Kingdom of God becomes the only agenda.

Recovering the dream

We often lament working with teachers who seem to have lost their imagination, lost the sense of why they chose education. If we can hold the big stories in front of them, show again the possibility of making a difference, remind them why they became teachers and why they became teachers in Catholic schools, we have the capacity to recapture their energy and their passion. This will be a significant bonus for the way they work, for the meaning they find or for the way they promote the Kingdom.

No one till someone believes in us

I have been blessed throughout my life to have people believe in me when I struggled for direction and purpose. I came across this quote from Dan Rather not so long ago:

> The dream begins most of the time with a teacher who believes in you, who tugs and pushes and leads you on to the next plateau, sometimes even poking you with a sharp stick called truth.

I was educated by the Christian Brothers until I finished Year 10. I was not a particularly good student but when I left St Paul's and went to Kempsey High School for Years 11 and 12, I became a worse student. So bad in fact that I didn't matriculate to any university or any tertiary program at the end of Year 12 – I failed the HSC! At that stage, my priorities in life were very different and revolved around the local beach culture. I attended school irregularly and had little motivation or interest.

When school finished, I went on the dole for six months and faced the embarrassment of seeing many of my friends coming and going from university for their breaks and holidays. Meanwhile, I read Wilbur Smith books and surfed!

After some prodding from my parents, I eventually took a job in a bank. It wasn't a bad job but at that time banks had a habit of moving young, single employees to inland country branches to 'do their time'. I had heard that a move for me had become imminent. This, to a coastal boy, was a very daunting prospect!

One Saturday morning, when I was walking down the main street of Kempsey, a Christian Brother who had taught me in my junior years approached me and asked me what I was doing with my life. Then Br Jim asked me a further question that changed my whole course in life.

He said, 'Wayne, have you ever thought about becoming a teacher?' I replied, 'Me, Brother, a teacher? Don't you know I didn't pass the HSC? I failed; I didn't matriculate to any university.' He said, 'Wayne I know this place in Sydney where we used to train brothers; we still do, but there aren't many of them. They're taking in lay people these days and perhaps if I put in a good word, we might be able to get you a start.'

It was really the last thing on my mind at that particular time. But a few weeks later, after hearing that my bank move out west was coming, I contacted Br Jim and asked if his offer was still on the table. He made a phone call to Br Dan Stewart. I was invited down to Strathfield for an interview, accepted into Mount St Mary College on probation and the rest, as they say, is history.

I share this story to remind you that you may never know fully the difference that you make in the lives of the young people you teach and form through your belief in them and their potential. The most profound difference you make as educators will be determined by your willingness to believe in the young. For some reason that I still don't understand, Brother Jim believed in me and said so. It made all the difference. The casual encounter where you show interest and concern may change someone's life. What a scary but magnificent possibility!

Who is your Teddy?

There is the magnificent story that educators have loved to tell for years. I have a colleague who has carried a copy of this story in his briefcase since it was given to him very early in his teaching career. That man, my great friend Ray Collins, is now a Diocesan Director of Catholic Education.

It is the story of a teacher named Mrs Thompson and her journey to belief in one of her students, Teddy Stoddart, whom she initially writes off but comes to inspire to reach his full potential. Mrs Thompson originally thought that Teddy's poor learning was due to his attitude and lack of interest. Upon perusing Teddy's records however, she learns that life has been tragic for Teddy and that just turning up at school is indeed a struggle. Her attitude changes, and it makes all the difference in Teddy's life. Through her belief in him, he goes on to achieve much in his life. If you haven't heard it, please

Google it or find a copy. It is the story of two people growing to full humanity through their belief in each other.

At the end of the story, at Teddy's wedding, they hugged each other and Teddy whispered in Mrs Thompson's ear, 'Thank you so much for making me feel important and showing me that I could make a difference.' Mrs Thompson, with tears in her eyes, whispered back, 'Teddy, you have it all wrong. You were the one who taught me that I could make a difference. I didn't know how to teach until I met you.'

Colleagues, let us never forget that our schools are filled with hundreds of 'Teddy Stoddarts', who need and crave our belief, attention and care in order to reach their full potential. Let us remember also that for the child in our care, who perhaps isn't so easy to like, we just may be his or her Mrs Thompson!

A future not our own

Recently on a plane flight, I saw the latest James Bond movie. In one scene I noticed that James was wearing a striped suit. Immediately some deep memories flooded back to me

Some time ago, when I was applying for a job which meant that I would have to move to the other side of the country, my dad noticed that the suit that I intended to wear to the interview was really not up to scratch. Dad had a keen eye, as for all of his working life he managed a menswear store. Dad didn't really want me to move states since he loved having family (especially grandchildren) around him. He had been alone for many years and was getting to the point of retirement. I guess this is fairly normal and natural.

To my surprise, just before I left for the interview, Dad asked me to try on a suit that he had bought for me, which he thought was far more presentable for the interview. I could sense his mixed feelings when he gave me the suit, which incidentally was a very similar design to the one James Bond wore in the movie – although I hope, nothing like the expense! I wore the suit at the interview and was fortunate enough to be offered the job. That suit then became my 'lucky suit', which I wore for many years subsequently at interviews and on other important occasions.

Dad knew that by giving me the suit he was increasing the possibility of my leaving him. A phrase is often attributed to Archbishop Romero; although there is some debate whether he actually said it, I like to think that he did. He spoke beautifully of the fact that, as ministers of the Gospel, we are prophets of a 'future not our own'.

As parents and educators we learn to let go and trust the future as we realize that the young people we nurture and form will leave us and travel different paths. We can't control what their destiny and contribution may be. We need to have confidence that we have played our part by doing what we can for them while they are in our care. We are called to educate for liberation. As such it calls us to free the emerging generation to fulfil their destiny in ways that we probably can't even imagine.

I think it was Joseph Campbell who suggested that the moment we begin nurturing the emerging generation, a part of us has to begin the process of dying, becoming less. This is the vocation of parenthood and the vocation of an educator.

I never cease to be inspired!

Who wouldn't be a teacher! I never cease to be inspired by the courageous stories I hear of the students in our schools.

The principal of a school that works closely with refugee students recently reported that a Year 11 boy had returned to school a week late after the summer holidays. When asked the reasons for his late arrival, the boy was at first reluctant to disclose. After some further prompting by the principal, the following story emerged.

This boy came from a proud refugee family. His family had struggled since arriving in Australia but prided themselves on doing their best to pay their way. After the boy had completed his studies the previous year, at the age of 16, he travelled alone to the country where he began a job picking fruit for the whole of the summer holidays. He returned home only for two days at Christmas time.

The reason why he needed the extra week before beginning

school was that he needed to work the extra days to complete the sum of money needed to pay for his following year's school fees. The principal was deeply moved when the boy proudly produced the entire year's school fees in cash — the fruits of his summer's work.

What inspiration!

Some messages for
the young

The trick will not desert you

In his book the *The Cruel Sea*, Nicholas Monsarrat writes about the sinking of a small ship called the *Compass Rose* during World War II.

Compass Rose had been sent to investigate a radar contact well behind the convoy and on her return to the main group of ships she was torpedoed. Monsarrat describes her sinking in graphic terms. It is his reference to how the men behave as they were thrown into the water that I would like to focus on.

Monsarrat comments that some men 'died well!' He contrasts these men to others who did not die so well and to others who gave up their lives without much of a struggle. He describes the ones who died well this way: 'These were the men who did all things well, automatically; in death, the trick did not desert them.'

Monsarrat then gives examples of how these men acted when the game was up and it was clear death was close. What they had in common was not heroics so much as a single-minded determination to keep doing their jobs —pushing others onto rafts, counting heads, passing out life jackets, staying on board a sinking ship to send distress signals and so forth. You can imagine the scene.

Michael Elphick highlights a key question which is a challenge to us all – what has this got to do with us? A war long ago, a scene few of us could ever expect to witness or experience? Most of us will never be called on to die in such a fashion, to meet such a moment – thank God! But perhaps we might be asked to *live* in such a fashion! Reflect again on the author's description of these men: 'These were the men who did all things well … in death the trick did not desert them.'

I think Monsarrat is saying that goodness is a habit, a practised act. It is something that is formed over a lifetime, the sum total of a lifetime of small choices in which the wellbeing of others is routinely put ahead of our own self-interest. So much so that when a moment of great challenge arrives, however unexpectedly, to do the right thing is an irresistible impulse, almost an instinct – the 'trick' or the habit does not desert you!

A meaningful life is made up of a series of daily acts of decency and kindness, which, ironically, over the course of a lifetime, add up to something truly great. Over two thousand years ago, Aristotle reminded people that we are what we repeatedly do. Excellence is not an act but a habit!

Small things – great love

Let us not forget this simple human wisdom: the road to happiness lies not through continual promoting our own self-interest but through living a life of service for others. Albert Schweitzer, the great thinker from the last century, said it this way: 'I don't know what your destiny will be but one thing I do know: The only ones among you who will be happy are those who have sought and found how to serve.'

For some this service might be on the 'big stage'. There are many people who will be formally recognized for their contribution to our nation. This is wonderful! But, for most of us, our contribution and service will be most needed and recognized in our families, friendship groups and local communities. No less important!

Mother Teresa reminded us that it is not how much we do, but how much love we put in the doing. It is not how much we give, but how much love we put in the giving. Her legacy can perhaps be summed up in her words: 'We need not do great things; only small things with great love.'

Our world desperately needs heroes. However, heroism does not require us to live up to a larger-than-life image of the hero as superman or super-woman. Heroism is not showing that you can handle anything and everything that comes your way. Rather, it is doing your own part, however humble that might be. In the words of Mother Teresa: 'Small deeds done with great love.'

One shot

A world built on prestige and social status has distorted the true meaning of success. It is not what we have done that is important; it is whether or not anything we did was worth doing. Has it made a difference for others? The quality of success we experience in our life depends upon the tiny choices we make every minute of every hour of every day.

Given that our currency slowly but surely inflates, if we live long enough probably we will all finish up millionaires. But, as Phillip Adams reminded a graduation class once, the BRW Rich List fails to mention that many of our wealthiest people are among our loneliest and least loved. But no one will ever be a millionaire in hours! We all finish up having, at best, a few thousand truly meaningful hours. So let us not waste them.

Despite what many would like us to believe, we only get one shot at life so we need to make it count. Let's not play small – let's take the necessary risks! Don't give up, no matter how hard it gets! Be yourself! Dance to your own beat! Love and serve as abundantly as you can!

Our success

Achievement and success in a school will not be measured by exam results or university admission scores. The measure of success will be this: How well have we prepared students to meet the challenges to come? How strong is their resolve? How generous is their spirit? How willing are they to embrace a future with less materialism but with more of what matters?

In whatever walk of life they find themselves, whether they

walk a world stage or a more humble one, are they convinced that the only way forward for all of us is in a world dedicated to the common good over individual gain?

As parents and teachers, preparing young people for what comes is the great work of our lives. If we have not convinced them of the absolute necessity of living a life for others, then we have failed more than them — we have failed the future, and tomorrow will be a more dangerous place because of it.

Being me

Authenticity for any school or college won't come from copying or competing with any other. Even if it did this well, it would always be second best to the other school.

Authenticity is being true to your self: taking the values and attributes you admire in others but making them yours. Let us apply this to our own lives.

It can be tough for young people as they try to find out who they really are. I spent the first 18 years of my life trying to be other people. There was a fellow in my school called Michael. He was the coolest, the best sportsman, great with the girls, popular and a great guitar player. I really wanted to be just like Michael. I started playing the guitar and imitating Michael in every way I could but, despite all my efforts, I could only ever manage to be the second-best Michael.

However, what I eventually discovered was that no one can be Wayne Tinsey like I can! I may not be the coolest or most gifted person but being the very best Wayne Tinsey is my greatest gift to the world. As imperfect and mixed up as I am!

Slaying the dragon

Recently my young niece told me a classic story about a hero who went out to slay a dragon who was threatening his people's village. How do we become heroes, and what do we have to slay to make our contribution to the world?

We become heroes when we accept ourselves as we are, when we live our lives according to our deepest values, when we make our life choices based on these values. In short, we are heroes when we are authentic! Heroism requires us all to find the treasure of our true selves and to share that treasure with the community.

The heroic life does not require us to become something greater than we are. But it does require us to be faithful to our own authentic path. Heroes are those who have given their lives to something bigger than themselves. To do this we must slay the dragon of envy, the dragon of fear to be different, the dragon that tells us that near enough is good enough, the dragon that tells us that it's OK to live a copied, inauthentic life.

Someone wise once said that the purpose of life is to live a life of purpose. But in order to contribute to the world in a most powerful way we must first come to know who we really are as a human being.

At the end of our life we will find that the things we thought were the big things were actually the little things, and that all the things we thought were the little, unimportant things were actually the big, important ones. In the end, it won't be what we have done that is important. It will be whether or not anything we did was worth doing. Has it made a difference for others? The quality of success we will experience in life depends upon the tiny choices we make every minute of every hour of every day.

Not perfect – just authentic

As we appropriately acknowledge the authenticity of our school or college, let us commit to being the most authentic people we can be. This entails accepting ourselves, being true to ourselves and to the deepest hopes held for us by our families and our society, and giving ourselves in the service of others.

Our human condition gives us one huge concession – we don't have to be perfect, just the best we can!

Not perfect but truly authentic!
No one can ask more of any school.
No one can ask more of you!

DR WAYNE TINSEY has taught at all levels of Catholic education throughout Australia, as well as in India and Peru. He is currently the Executive Director of Edmund Rice Education Australia, a network of Catholic schools spanning every state and territory of Australia.

Prior to his current role, Wayne was Director of Schools in the Diocese of Maitland-Newcastle for four years. In 2007 the Catholic Education Commission of New South Wales awarded Wayne the Br John Taylor Award for Excellence in Education for his leadership and management of the schools in that diocese.

In the early 2000s, Wayne simultaneously held the positions of Director of the Catholic Institute of Western Australia, Director of the Edmund Rice Centre for Social Justice, Head of the School of Religious Education, as well as Professor and Assistant Dean of Education at the University of Notre Dame in Fremantle. Recently he was asked to be the inaugural Chair of *Edmund Rice Education beyond Borders*, a global community of some 250 schools dedicated to justice, liberation and an option for the marginalized.

All this being said, these days Wayne prefers to be known as a husband, parent and educator who strives to grow in deeper awareness of the blessings, challenges and responsibilities that come with these most privileged of roles.

www.ingramcontent.com/pod-product-compliance
Lightning Source LLC
Chambersburg PA
CBHW071354080526
44587CB00017B/3106